pathway to prayer

encouragements to pray

—— *from* ——

voices of the past

M.J. Hancock, Editor

To Paul & Carol Schmidt
who like Epaphras
have struggled on our behalf
in their prayers

CruciformPress

CruciformPress.com | info@CruciformPress.com

"Hancock has gathered a treasury of quotations pertinent to a difficult and challenging subject: the practice of prayer. This is a book to read slowly and meditatively, as each quotation is a sword to cut down our pride, a burning coal to ignite our hearts with holy desire, and a compass to direct us in the way of communion with God."

Dr. Joel R. Beeke, President, Puritan Reformed Theological Seminary, Grand Rapids, Michigan

"I have often thought it would be a good idea to compile a collection of quotes from godly saints of the past on the topic of prayer specifically. What we have here in this book is exactly what I had in mind, beautifully and comprehensively realized. Today's church has become expert in so many things that she may be tempted to disparage any instruction from a former generation. But that would be a great error. Our forefathers, though more primitive in their tools, excelled where it mattered most. Namely, in the place of prayer. Let us have the humility to recognize our poverty in this vital Christian virtue and seek by God's help to recover that which has largely been lost. Read this book slowly and thoughtfully as every single quote deserves our careful attention. May the Lord be pleased to revive the art of soul communion within the heart of every child of God."

Steven Lee, Founder, Sermon Audio

"When my colleague asked if I would write something in support of this new compendium on prayer, it came into my mind in one terrifying moment that he somehow knew the truth about my private prayer life, and that his scheme was to get me to read this book and be changed. If that was his scheme, it was brilliantly successful. I expected to be convicted by the exhortations of my older brothers and sisters—and they indeed left marks. What I didn't expect was the warm encouragement from those same brothers and sisters, their own confessions of struggle in prayer, and their down-to-earth ideas for bringing about a real change of heart and habit. As I made mark after mark on my copy, the passages made mark after mark on my own soul. I was being changed.

"I'm pretty sure that I'm not the only one who desperately needs the transforming encouragements of this book."

J.D. Crowley, Ratanakiri, Cambodia

M.J. Hancock lives with his wife and six children in Cambodia where they have served as missionaries since 2014.

Pathway to Prayer: Encouragements to Pray from Voices of the Past

Print / PDF ISBN: 978-1-949253-42-9
Mobipocket ISBN: 978-1-949253-44-3
ePub ISBN: 978-1-949253-43-6

Contents

Four: Steps after Prayer

Part II: Approaching the Triune God in Prayer

Five: Praying to the Father

Six: Praying through the Son

Seven: Praying in the Spirit

Foreword

It wouldn't quite be right to say that John Piper taught me the importance of a good quote, but it might be fair to say that he helped me better understand why I'm so drawn to them. "Books don't change people, paragraphs do—sometimes sentences," he says. And it has often been my experience that if I read an entire book and, at the end of it all, remember one particularly good sentence, I am well satisfied.

This is a book of quotes that concern an especially important subject. Prayer is the duty and delight of every Christian, yet one that we all know to be especially difficult. Though we know that prayer is one of the keys to spiritual life and health, we also know that we are only ever students in the school of prayer, children who know our Father gives us good gifts when we ask, yet children who sometimes doubt that he really will.

Quotes plus prayer, then, is an especially helpful combination. *Pathway to Prayer* contains hundreds of quotes from fellow Christians—quotes that are meant to help you better understand why you must pray and how to pray and, perhaps best of all, quotes meant to help you to actually pray.

As you read this book, I suggest you discipline yourself to savor it—to read it slowly and meditatively. Though you could probably read it from cover to cover in a couple of hours, I believe you will find the greater benefit in treating each of these quotes as an opportunity to think, to pray, to listen, and to learn.

Read each paragraph or sentence with patience, expecting these brief but dense summaries of truth to lead you deeper into your relationship with the Lord who commands and invite us to pray.

Tim Challies
Ontario, Canada

Preface

Many have found prayer to be the most difficult exercise in the Christian life. It seems that a host of internal and external forces are busily engaged to dissuade us, distract us, and discourage us from praying. We can see from the writings of Christians from previous generations that they too struggled to pray. But we can also observe how the Lord helped many of them find the way over the hurdles until prayer became a delightful privilege and determined practice in their lives. Certainly, these former men and women of prayer could provide tremendous help to us today in our struggle to pray if their insightful teaching, practical advice, and stirring exhortations were collected, organized, and made accessible to us.

This is why *Pathway to Prayer* was compiled, to provide today's readers with a treasure trove of encouragement to pray from a broad collection of voices from the past. More than five hundred quotations from over one hundred authors have been selected and organized into both practical and theological topics of prayer. The first part of the book lays out practical steps to follow in order to move forward in prayer and overcome the common hurdles. The second part presents the vital work of our triune God, so active and eager to encourage and empower our praying.

You will probably find this book most useful if you work through it slowly in quiet moments of reflection, especially preceding a time of planned prayer. As Richard Baxter recommended, "Reading over some part of a warm and quickening book, will do much to warm and quicken a benumbed soul … and put life into us before we address ourselves more nearly unto God." I have asked the Lord to make this collection one such warm and life-giving book that he repeatedly uses to melt away our aversion and apathy toward prayer, rekindle our desire and determination for prayer, empower our resistance to every hindrance to prayer, and ultimately lead us to pray, to really draw near to God and speak to him. Ponder through these pages with a teachable spirit, and you will find your heart prepared and prompted to pray.

Father, you have told me to keep on praying and never give up (Luke 18:1), yet consistent prayer remains such a struggle. You know all the hardships I've faced in prayer and all the times I've walked away from you into seasons of prayerlessness. But you are merciful and gracious, so you keep bringing me back to the path of prayer, making the way clear through the teaching and encouragement of my brothers and sisters. Thank you for their biblical instruction and practical advice, their honesty in sharing their struggles, and their testimonies of your faithfulness in helping them overcome. And now I ask you Lord, by your Spirit, continue to use these writings to lead others down this pathway to prayer into a fuller knowledge of you. Answer me for the spiritual renewal of your people and the advance of Christ's kingdom among all the peoples of the earth. I ask through the name of your beloved Son and my Savior, Jesus Christ.

> *Come, and stir us up to pray;*
> *wake us from our slumber.*
> *Fill us with love and zeal that cries;*
> *then send down your answer.*

M.J. Hancock
Tbong Khmum, Cambodia

Part I

Taking Steps Forward in Prayer

Therefore, since we are surrounded by so great a cloud of witnesses, let us also lay aside every weight, and sin which clings so closely, and let us run with endurance the race that is set before us, looking to Jesus, the founder and perfecter of our faith. (Heb. 12:1-2)

Look to Jesus, for he has left you an example that you should tread in his steps. His life is a living rule to his people; besides Christ's example ... you have a cloud of witnesses, ... men of like passions, temptations, and constitutions with you .... [And] where they followed Christ and kept the way, they are [proposed] for your imitation.[1]

~John Flavel (c.1627-1691)

Listen carefully to the witnesses lining our path. They have much to offer us: their *encouragements* embolden us to pray; their *exhortations* arouse us to pray; their *advice* and *teachings* inform us to pray; their *confessions of weakness* console us to pray; their *testimonies of grace* assure us to pray; and their *exemplary lives* inspire us to pray. (cf. Psa. 66:16-19; Heb. 10:24-25; Jam. 5:16-17)[2]

~Anonymous

[They] seem to say, "Imitate our example, and yours will be our reward. Will you linger where we hastened? Flee where we fought? Fall where we stood? Surrender where we conquered?

Oh! be not slothful, but [follow] us, who through faith and patience, are inheriting the promises." [3]

~Octavius Winslow (1808-1878)

Now, though we [may] have nothing of our own experience to support us, yet the remembrance of what has been done for others, the experiences of the saints ... are set down for our learning, for the support of our faith and hope (cf. Rom. 15:4). They trusted in God, and found him a ready help; why may not we? ... The experience of others, not in one, but in every age ... is for the [encouragement] and instruction of the church. [4]

~Thomas Manton (1620-1677)

In you our fathers trusted; they trusted, and you delivered them. To you they cried and were rescued. (Psa. 22:4-5)

One

Initial Steps Toward Prayer

† † †

Set Your Heart to Seek the Lord

What are you seeking? † Now set your mind and heart to seek the
LORD your God. (John 1:38; 1 Chr. 22:19)

The indispensable requisite for all true praying is a deeply seated
desire which seeks after God himself. [1]

~ *E.M. Bounds (1835-1913)*

Communion with God is the one need of the soul beyond all
other needs, [and] prayer is the beginning of that communion. [2]

~ *James Hastings (1852-1922)*

[Only] in union and communion with [God], will the longings
of the immortal spirit be at length fully and forever satisfied. [3]

~ *John MacDuff (1818-1895)*

There is in the heart of man such a drought, without this River
of paradise, that all the waters in the world, though every drop
were an ocean, cannot quench it …. Augustine said, "Lord, you

have made our heart for you, and it will never rest till it come
to you."[4]

~*George Swinnock (1627-1673)*

The heart of man must have an object unto which it is inclined
or upon which it does cleave; for it is like a sponge, that being
thirsty in itself, sucks in moisture from other things; it is a chaos
of desires, seeking to be filled with something from without.
We were made for another, to be happy in the enjoyment of a
being [outside of ourselves] …. We all hunt about for a match
for our affections, for some good to satisfy us.[5]

~*Thomas Manton (1620-1677)*

We were made for God, and can never enjoy satisfaction until
we come to enjoy him …. [So let] the chiefest Good be sought
after with the chiefest care, and chiefest love, and chiefest
delight.[6]

~*Thomas Manton (1620-1677)*

The whole spiritual life is but a pursuit of the soul towards God;
and the more constantly and earnestly we seek him … the more
we have of the love of God in us. Therefore, David expresses
this desire, as exceeding all other desires: "One thing have I desired of the Lord, that will I seek after, that I might dwell in the
house of the Lord all the days of my life, to behold the beauty of
the Lord, and to inquire in his temple" (Psa. 27:4).[7]

~*Thomas Manton (1620-1677)*

There were other things David might desire, but his heart was
set upon this *one thing*, that he might enjoy constant communion with God.[8]

~*Thomas Manton (1620-1677)*

Oh! I thirst, I pant, I gasp after him, I long for communion and
peace with him; with my soul do I desire you in the night, yes,
with my spirit within me do I seek you early. (Isa. 26:9)[9]

~*Isaac Ambrose (1604-1664)*

Come near to the holy men and women of the past and you will soon feel the heat of their desire after God. They mourned for him, they prayed and wrestled and sought for him day and night, in season and out, and when they had found him, the finding was all the sweeter for the long seeking.[10]

~ *A. W. Tozer (1897-1963)*

As a deer pants for flowing streams, so pants my soul for you, O God. My soul thirsts for God, for the living God † O God, you are my God; earnestly I seek you; my soul thirsts for you; my flesh faints for you, as in a dry and weary land where there is no water. (Psa. 42:1-2; 63:10)

David's life was a torrent of spiritual desire, and his psalms ring with the cry of the seeker and the glad shout of the finder. Paul confessed the mainspring of his life to be his burning desire after Christ. *That I may know him* was the goal of his heart, and to this he sacrificed everything.[11]

~ *A. W. Tozer (1897-1963)*

In what channel does the stream of your desires run? ... What is the calling which you [pursue] with greatest eagerness and earnestness? ... The Christian, who has the blessed God for his portion, strives and labors, and watches and prays, and mourns, and thinks no time too much, no pains too great, no cost enough for the enjoyment of his God.[12]

~*George Swinnock (1627-1673)*

Draw more near to God every day in a holy communion, and you shall have more grace from him .... You have the promises, "Turn unto me, and I will turn unto you," and "Return unto me, and I will return unto you" (Zech. 1:3; Mal. 3:7).[13]

~*Edward Bickersteth (1786-1850)*

Draw near to God, and he will draw near to you. † The Lord is near to all who call on him. † The Lord is good ... to the soul who seeks him. † Those who seek the Lord

lack no good thing. † *Whoever would draw near to God
must believe that he exists and that he rewards those who
seek him.* † *It is good for me to draw near God.* (Jam. 4:8;
Psa. 145:8; Lam. 3:25; Heb. 11:6; Psa. 73:28 KJV)

I thirst, I long to know more of him. I feel that all I have ever
known of him is like the whispering of the sea in the shell, while
the awful roar of the sea itself has not yet reached my ears ....
Oh, I long to plunge into the sea itself, to bathe myself in the
broad ocean of his infinite generosity and love to me. [14]

~ *C.H. Spurgeon (1834-1892)*

Jesus, thou Joy of loving hearts, thou Fount of life, thou Light
of men, From the best bliss that earth imparts we turn unfilled
to thee again .... We taste thee, O thou Living Bread, and long
to feast upon thee still: We drink of thee, the Fountainhead and
thirst our souls from thee to fill. [15]

~*Bernard of Clairvaux (c. 1090-1153)*

O God, I have tasted your goodness, and it has both satisfied
me and made me thirsty for more. I am painfully conscious of
my need of further grace. I am ashamed of my lack of desire. O
God, the triune God, I want *to want* you; I long to be *filled with
longing*; I thirst to be *made more thirsty* still. Show me your
glory, I pray you, that so I may know you indeed. [16]

~ *A.W. Tozer (1897-1963)*

O that [my heart] would vent itself with mighty longings, and
infinite aspirations after this blessed object! Lord, I desire, but
help my faint desires; blow on my dying spark, it is but little ....
O that my spark would flame! Lord, I desire that I might desire;
O breathe it into me, and I will desire you. [17]

~*Isaac Ambrose (1604-1664)*

O gracious God, be pleased to pardon all the defects of my love
to you, and all the excesses of my love to earthly things; and
turn my inclinations and affections from all vain objects to your

blessed self, who is most worthy of all my love .... Touch my heart with such a powerful sense of your loveliness and your lovingkindness, that I may experience stronger desires and inclinations after you, and greater [satisfaction] and delight in you .... O give me the grace and the power to love you. Let me be ever longing to appear before you, and [be] delighting in the duties that bring me near to you, and that help me to communion with you. [18]

~Benjamin Jenks (1646-1724)

How lovely is your dwelling place, O Lord of hosts! My soul longs, yes, faints for the courts of the Lord. (Psa. 84:1-2)

My Lord and my God, whom have I in heaven but you? And there is none upon earth that I desire besides you (Psa. 73:25). O be not as a stranger to [my] soul ... but bless and honor me with that divine fellowship of which you have made me capable, and which my soul pants after .... Yes, give me grace, O my Lord, to go on seeking till I find you, whom my soul desires above all to love. [19]

~Benjamin Jenks (1646-1724)

† † †

Recommit to Following Christ's Example

If anyone serves me, he must follow me. † Take my yoke upon you, and learn from me. (John 12:26; Matt. 11:29)

"Learn of me," says Christ .... Let us follow him. Does Christ pray? Let us pray. Does he pray for us and others? Let us pray for ourselves, and then let us pray for one another. [20]

~Isaac Ambrose (1604-1664)

The highest way of honoring Christ is to be like to Christ; he who says he abides in him, ought himself also to walk even as he walked. (1 John 2:6)[21]

~Thomas Brooks (1608-1680)

[Whoever] is not leading a life of prayer, no matter how many excellent things he may be doing, is not walking as Jesus walked. [22]

~R.A. Torrey (1856-1928)

Our Lord's life was exceptionally busy. He worked under constant pressure. At times he had no leisure even for meals, but the pressure of the multitudes was never permitted to crowd out prayer. (cf. Luke 4:42; 5:16)[23]

~J. Oswald Sanders (1902-1992)

And rising very early in the morning, while it was still dark, he departed and went out to a desolate place, and there he prayed. (Mark 1:35)

We may say his whole life was a kind of prayer, a constant course of communion with God. If the sacrifice was not always offering, yet was the fire still kept alive. [24]

~Henry Scougal (1650-1678)

Let our Lord's conduct … be our example. We cannot work miracles as he did; in this he stands alone. But we can walk in his steps, in the matter of private devotion. If we have the Spirit of adoption, we can pray. Let us resolve to pray more than we have done hitherto. Let us strive to make time and place and opportunity for being alone with God. [25]

~J.C. Ryle (1816-1900)

He did not spend one moment of time unprofitably in over thirty years. How early does he rise, and how earnestly does he pursue this business of communion with his Father in the work of our redemption? … [Here is] a pattern for our imitation ….

He prayed, so that we might pray and reap the profit of all his prayers and purchase. [26]

~*Oliver Heywood (1630-1702)*

Wise will it be for us to consider Jesus …. If he, the sinless One, he the mighty One, he the divine One, felt deeply and momentarily the need of drawing from above by the breath of prayer those supplies needful for the accomplishment of his work and for the glorifying of his Father, oh, how much more have we need that prayer should precede, accompany, and follow every step we take; that communion with God should prompt, aid, and sanctify every act of our lives; that, in a word, in imitation of our blessed Lord, we should often rise up a great while before day, and depart into a solitary place, and before secular and worldly things took possession of our minds, give ourselves to prayer. [27]

~*Octavius Winslow (1808-1878)*

Oh that we would daily propound to ourselves this noble pattern for our imitation, and make it our business, our work, our heaven, to write after this blessed copy that Christ has set us, namely, to be much with God alone. [28]

~*Thomas Brooks (1608-1680)*

O thou, by whom we come to God, the Life, the Truth, the Way, The path of prayer thyself hast trod, Lord, teach us how to pray. [29]

~*James Montgomery (1771-1854)*

† † †

Acknowledge the Difficulty

And he told them a parable to the effect that they ought always to pray and not lose heart. (Luke 18:1)

Though in its beginnings prayer is so simple that the feeblest child can pray, yet it is at the same time the highest and holiest work to which man can rise. [30]

~Andrew Murray (1828-1917)

[Here] is something we all have learned from experience: there is nothing in a sense which is so difficult as just to pray. There are many difficulties [in it] …. These things tend to happen because prayer is the supreme activity of the human soul. It is the highest point we ever reach in this life, communion with God. As we engage in prayer, all the forces of hell are playing upon us, and they are doing their utmost to spoil our efforts …. Don't be discouraged by the fact that you have found prayer difficult. [31]

~Martyn Lloyd-Jones (1899-1981)

Sometimes it may seem to us that our prayer life would develop more easily under easier conditions, [but] the open field with no obstacle … carries no exhilaration. [32]

~Amy Carmichael (1867-1951)

Prayer comes by training, and there is no discipline so exacting …. It is the very highest energy of which the human heart is capable, and it calls for the total concentration of all the faculties. [33]

~Samuel Chadwick (1860-1932)

[Prayer] is a travail and not a pastime. If it were easy it might scarcely be worth counseling: it is tremendously difficult, but its rewards are infinite. [34]

~J.H. Jowett (1864-1923)

To speak especially of the lack of prayer, and the desire of living a fuller prayer-life, how many are the difficulties …. We have so often resolved to pray more and better and have failed. We have not the strength of will some have, with one resolve to turn round and change our habits. The press of duty is as great as it ever was; it is so difficult to find time for more prayer … [and] our prayers, instead of being a joy and a strength, are a source of continual self-condemnation and doubt. We have at times mourned and confessed and resolved; but, to tell the honest truth, we do not expect, for we do not see the way to any great change. [35]

~Andrew Murray (1828-1917)

As long as we measure our power for praying aright and perseveringly by what we feel, or think we can accomplish, we shall be discouraged when we hear of how much we ought to pray. But when we quietly believe that, in the midst of all our conscious weakness, the Holy Spirit as a Spirit of supplication is dwelling within us, for the very purpose of enabling us to pray in such manner and measure as God would have us, our hearts will be filled with hope. [36]

~Andrew Murray (1828-1917)

Through the mercy of the Father, the merit of the mediating Son, and the might of the inspiring Spirit, prayer is possible …. [If] we understand to whom, and through whom, and by whom we pray, our praying will become prevailing. [37] (cf. Part 2: Approaching the Triune God in Prayer)

~G. Campbell Morgan (1863-1945)

[O Lord], we bewail our coldness, our poverty, our empty hearts, our selfish desires, our languid services, our prayerless prayers, our praiseless praises. How different are we from what we desire to be! How different are we from what we might be! Come, Holy Spirit …. Arise in our behalf. Come forth to our help. Put forth your strength to bless and save us. And to your great name, Father, Son, and Holy Spirit, be everlasting praise! [38]

~Henry Law (1797-1884)

† † †

Acknowledge Your Helplessness

But I, O LORD, cry to you; in the morning my prayer comes before you .... I am helpless. (Psa. 88:13-15)

[We are not] sufficient of ourselves, our sufficiency is of God; therefore, there is a necessity of daily [communion] with God ... and of waiting at his gate; as the beggar, who has neither a bit of bread, nor a penny to buy any [waits] at the rich man's door for supply. Our spiritual strength is like Israel's manna, rained down daily; we are kept by a divine power, and allowed but from hand to mouth, that we might continually depend on, and resort to, the Lord Jesus for our allowance. [39]

~George Swinnock (1627-1673)

Christ does not teach you to pray, "Lord, give me enough to serve me for two or three years" but, "this day our daily bread." This is to teach us that we must live upon God in a dependent condition every day. [40]

~Jeremiah Burroughs (1599-1646)

[Our] spirits daily are decaying, and if not daily renewed by proper nourishment we perish. The vessels that are always leaking, must stand constantly under the conduit to get what they lose. [41]

~George Swinnock (1627-1673)

We are always needing; and therefore, we need to be praying always. The world is always alluring; and therefore, we need to be always praying. Satan is always tempting; and therefore, we need to be always praying. We are always sinning; and therefore, we need to be always praying. We are in dangers always; and therefore, we need to be praying always. [42]

~Thomas Brooks (1608-1680)

To pray is nothing more involved than ... giving Jesus access to our needs, and permitting him to exercise his own power in dealing with them .... And that requires no strength. It is only a question of our wills. Will we give Jesus access to our needs?[43]

~O. Hallesby (1879-1961)

[People] sit down groaning under their discouragements because they do not look further than themselves .... God humbles us with much weakness, that he may [turn us to] prayer .... If God commands anything above [our natural ability], it is to bring [us to our] knees for grace.[44]

~Thomas Manton (1620-1677)

The Christian often tries to forget his weakness; God wants us to remember it, to feel it deeply .... The Christian thinks his weaknesses are his greatest hindrance in the life and service of God; God tells us that it is the secret of strength and success. It is our weakness, heartily accepted and continually realized, that gives our claim and access to the strength of him who has said, "My strength is made perfect in weakness" (2 Cor. 12:9).[45]

~Andrew Murray (1828-1917)

The Lord humbles and brings us low in our own eyes, and shows us our misery and sinful poverty, and that in us is no good thing, that we be stripped of all helps in and without ourselves (cf. Luke 8:43) .... [Yet our extremity] is the means to bring us to Christ, to drive us on our knees, helpless [and] low as may be—to show us where [the] only help is to be found and make us run into it.[46]

~Richard Sibbes (1577-1635)

Prayer is not the work of the memory and wit, but the proper work of a broken heart.[47]

~John Preston (1587-1628)

When the poor and needy seek water, and there is none, and their tongue is parched with thirst, I the Lord will answer them. (Isa. 41:17)

The utterly weak cry out unto God as nobody else does. He is too weak to play at praying: he groans, he sighs, he weeps. In his abject weakness he prevails as Jacob did …. He falls; and as he falls, he grasps his antagonist and holds him fast, crying, … "I cannot wrestle with you; I cannot try another fall. But I *can* and *will* hold you fast. The dead weight of my weakness makes me hold you as an anchor holds a ship. I will not let you go except you bless me."[48]

~C.H. Spurgeon (1834-1892)

Let me persuade you to make a full confession of weakness to the Lord. Say, "Lord, I cannot do what I *ought* to do: I cannot do what I *want* to do: I cannot do what I *used* to do: I cannot do what *other people* do: I cannot do what I *mean* to do: I cannot do what I am *sure I shall* do: I cannot do what I *feel impelled* to do; and over this sinful weakness I mourn." Then add, "Lord, I long to serve you perfectly, yet I cannot do it … unless you continue to fill me with your own holy energy. Lord, help me! Lord, help me!"[49]

~C.H. Spurgeon (1834-1892)

As for me, I am poor and needy, but the Lord takes thought for me. You are my help and my deliverer. † Behold, God is my helper; the Lord is the upholder of my life. † [He] daily bears us up. (Psa. 40:17; 54:4; 68:19)

Can we find a friend so faithful who will all our sorrows share? Jesus knows our every weakness; take it to the Lord in prayer! Are we weak and heavy laden, cumbered with a load of care? Precious Savior, still our refuge—take it to the Lord in prayer![50]

~Joseph Scriven (1819-1886)

[O Lord], you know our infirmities—let your strength be made perfect in our weakness. Our duties are far above our own power—let your grace be sufficient for us. Our dangers are numberless, and we are utterly unable to keep ourselves from falling—hold us up, and we shall be safe. The burdens we feel would press our lives down to the ground—lay underneath us your everlasting arms. [51]

~William Jay (1769-1853)

† † †

Examine Your Prayer Life

Let us test and examine our ways, and return to the LORD! Let us lift up our hearts and hands to God in heaven. (Lam. 3:40-41)

It would be well for us all, if we examined ourselves more frequently as to our habits about private prayer. What time do we give to it in the twenty-four hours of the day? What progress can we mark, one year with another, in the fervency, fullness, and earnestness of our prayers? What do we know by experience of, "laboring fervently in prayer?" (Col. 4:12). These are humbling inquiries, but they are useful for our souls. [52]

~J.C. Ryle (1816-1900)

In the morning was especially impressed with the awful fact that by losing one hour of prayer every day by not rising early, I lost twenty days of prayer in the course of a year. [53]

~Andrew Bonar (1810-1892)

O how precious is time! And how ... I have trifled it away and not improved it. [How I have] neglected to fill up each part of it with [prayer] to the utmost of my ability and capacity. [54]

~David Brainerd (1718-1747)

It is my deepest regret that I pray so little. I should count the days ... by the times I have been enabled to pray in faith, and to take hold upon God. [55]

~Andrew Bonar (1810-1892)

I see that prayerlessness is one of my great sins of omission. I am too short, ask too little, ask with too much [lack] of forethought [and with] too little meditation upon Scripture. [56]

~Andrew Bonar (1810-1892)

Oh, let us keep an eye continually upon our private devotions! Here is the pith, and marrow, and backbone of our practical Christianity. [57]

~J.C. Ryle (1816-1900)

O reader, reflect upon your duties [of prayer], consider what spirituality, sincerity, humility, broken-heartedness, and melting affections after God, are to be found in your duties: Is it so with you? Or do you hurry over your duties as all interruption to your business and pleasures? Are they an ungrateful task, imposed upon you by God, and your own conscience? Are there no hungerings and thirstings after God in your soul? [58]

~John Flavel (c.1627-1691)

Godly men go no further than their own closets for the proof of their depravity. [59]

~Alexander Whyte (1836-1921)

Watch and pray that you may not enter into temptation. The spirit indeed is willing, but the flesh is weak. (Matt. 26:41)

Backsliding generally first begins with *neglect of private prayer* .... The daily act of prayer itself is hurried over, or gone through without the heart: these are the kind of downward steps which many a Christian descends to a condition of spiritual palsy, or reaches the point where God allows him to have a tremendous fall. [60]

~J.C. Ryle (1816-1900)

O guard against it, reader; look well to the state of your soul; examine your prayers; see that you have not substituted the cold *form* for the glowing *spirit*, the mere body for the soul. Real prayer is the breathing of God's own Spirit in the heart; have you *this*? It is *communion* and *fellowship* with God; know you what *this* is? It is brokenness, contrition, confession, and that often springing from an overwhelming sense of his goodness and his love shed abroad in the heart; is *this* your experience? Again, we repeat it, look well to your prayers. [61]

~Octavius Winslow (1808-1878)

Have you forgotten the chamber, the closet, the barn, or the forest where you sometimes walked and meditated? ... How did it come to pass that there has been such a change; that you go so rarely to visit your best friend as you did previously? [62]

~Oliver Heywood (1630-1702)

Where is the blessedness I knew when first I sought the Lord? Where is the soul-refreshing view of Jesus and his word?

What peaceful hours I then enjoyed! How sweet their memory still!

But they have left an aching void the world can never fill.

Return, O Holy Dove, return, sweet messenger of rest; I hate the sins that made thee mourn, and drove thee from my breast. [63]

~William Cowper (1731-1800)

[O Lord], we look back on the past hours, and we are conscious of broken vows, lack of true service, backsliding steps, and unfaithful words. Crowds of vain thoughts and worthless works accuse us. Enter not into judgment with your faithless servants.

We confess our manifold shortcomings. [Only by the] merits of your beloved Son, cleanse us from all unrighteousness. Cast our sins and our iniquities behind your back. Bury them in the ocean of Jesus' blood. [64]

~Henry Law (1797-1884)

† † †

Confess Sin

If I had cherished iniquity in my heart, the Lord would not have listened. But truly God has listened. (Psa. 66:18-19)

If prayer does not constantly endeavor the ruin of sin, sin will ruin prayer, and utterly alienate the soul from it. [65]

~John Owen (1616-1683)

If I permit sin to lodge in my heart—and no sin can do so without my consent—if I side with it, and do not rather resist it ... and cast it out, then the word of God loses its edge and prayer is restrained. [66]

~Gordon Watt (1865-1928)

When the sin of the petitioner is before God's eyes, his petitions cannot enter into God's ears; the wide mouth of sin outcries the voice of his prayers .... The smallest sin, loved and liked, will hinder the course of prayer, though it be never so instant and vehement. The Lord's ear is not [deaf] that it cannot hear, but your iniquities [have made a separation] between you and your God. (Isa. 59:1-2) [67]

~George Swinnock (1627-1673)

When a sick man is in a decline, his lungs suffer, and his voice, and so when a Christian is in a spiritual decline, the breath of prayer is affected, and the cry of supplication becomes weak

.... [If] your prayers are hindered, there is something in your spiritual system which needs to be ejected or something lacking which ought to be taken care of at once! [68]

~C.H. Spurgeon (1834-1892)

If there is any sin or dispute that is constantly coming up in your moments of close communion with God, that is the thing that hinders prayer; put it away. [69]

~R.A. Torrey (1856-1928)

The dearest idol I have known, whate'er that idol be, help me to tear it from thy throne and worship only thee. [70]

~William Cowper (1731-1800)

Beloved, let us search and try our ways, and turn again unto the Lord. Let us be willing to say, "Search me, O God, and know my heart; try me and know my ways, and see if there be any wicked way in me, and lead me in the way everlasting" (Psa. 139:23-24). [71]

~A.B. Simpson (1843-1919)

"Search me, O God."... Commit [this] prayer to memory. Pray it daily, constantly, and let the Searcher of hearts have his way with you at whatever cost. The searching may be bitter, but the end will be sweet. [72]

~John Hyde (1865-1912)

[When] God searches the heart as with eyes of flame, and brings to our conscience things long buried in oblivion, and enables us to search and try our ways and lay open all our heart before him, then we may receive his blessing unhindered and unbounded and know the blessedness of the man whose transgression is forgiven, whose sin is covered and in whose spirit there is no [deceit]. (Psa. 32:1-2) [73]

~A.B. Simpson (1843-1919)

Heavenly Father, ... we cloak not our wretchedness. Our lips are ready to confess—but our hearts are slow to feel, and our

feet are reluctant to amend our ways. We bring our hard hearts
unto you. Break them by your Spirit—and then bind them up
by your grace. Wound them to the core—and then pour in the
Gospel-balm. Such is the blindness of our fallen nature—that
we cannot see sin's deformity, except as you are pleased to un-
mask it. Such is our deadness—that we cannot hate it, except
as you shall graciously implant abhorrence. Such is our infirmity—that we cannot flee it, except as your strength enables.
Conscious of all inability, we come to you for light, for help, for
strength, for blessing. [74]

~Henry Law (1797-1884)

Gracious Lord Jesus, ... may your pierced hand take of your
own blood and obliterate the record of this day's sins .... We
plead the heaven-sent promise, "If we confess our sins, he is
faithful and just to forgive us our sins, and to cleanse us from all
unrighteousness" (1 John 1:9). [75]

~Henry Law (1797-1884)

† † †

Reconcile with Others

So if you ... remember that your brother has something against you,
leave your gift there before the altar and go. First be reconciled to
your brother, and then come and offer your gift. (Matt. 5:23-24)

The spirit of cherished animosity, lurking prejudice, sullen
vindictiveness, or cold disdain will as effectively obstruct our
intercourse and intimacy with heaven as a speck upon the crys-
talline lens of the eye will obstruct our vision, or the crossing of
the wires of the electric machinery of a building will leave us in
darkness. [76]

~A. B. Simpson (1843-1919)

Beloved, is this hindering your prayers? Can you think this moment of some brother or sister from whom you are wrongly estranged; some person whom you treat with studied harshness, neglect, perhaps disdain, or possibly with injury and injustice; some word that you have spoken against your brother, and which you should not have spoken even if true; some word to which you have listened against your brother, and never should have heard except in his presence; some cherished suspicion, criticism, or judgment where you have no business even to think evil? May God help you to see the way to discover some cause of unanswered prayer![77]

~A.B. Simpson (1843-1919)

Be honest! Look at the matter, however distasteful and painful it may be, fairly, fully in the face. Has any relation, Christian brother or sister, offended, injured, wounded you? ... Are there any with whom you are not upon good and friendly terms? Do you meet in society, pass each other in the street, worship in the same sanctuary, and approach the same sacred table of the Lord's Supper without friendly recognition, or Christian communion? ... And must this painful state of things exist?[78]

~Octavius Winslow (1808-1878)

[No, it] need not and must not continue. In his Name who, when we were sinners, loved us ... I beseech you, before the sun shall go down upon your wrath, seek out the brother or the sister whom you have offended, or who has offended you, and hold out your hand of reconciliation.[79]

~Octavius Winslow (1808-1878)

Forgive us our debts, as we also have forgiven our debtors .... For if you forgive others their trespasses, your heavenly Father will also forgive you, but if you do not forgive others their trespasses, neither will your Father forgive your trespasses. For if you forgive others their trespasses, your heavenly Father will also forgive you, but if you do not

*forgive others their trespasses, neither will your Father
forgive your trespasses. (Matt. 6:12, 14-15)*

[O Lord], pardon any who may have injured me, and if I have
injured any, may I be ready to confess my fault, and to make
restitution for any wrong done, and may they be disposed to
forgive me. [80]

~William Jay (1769-1853)

✝ ✝ ✝

Resist the Flesh

*The desires of the flesh are against the Spirit, and the desires of the
Spirit are against the flesh, for these are opposed to each other, to keep
you from doing the things you want to do. ✝ Beloved, I urge you as
sojourners and exiles to abstain from the passions of the flesh, which
wage war against your soul. (Gal. 5:17; 1 Pet. 2:11)*

The flesh is really our enemy; yes, our greatest enemy. Therefore we should not indulge the flesh, but give up ourselves to
be ruled by the Spirit …. When we are [engaged in spiritual]
duties, the flesh distracts us with vain thoughts …. [It] makes
us drowsy, dead-hearted, and weary of God's service …. [It]
makes us lazy and negligent, and diverts us by proposals … that
we have no time nor heart for God. [81]

~Thomas Manton (1620-1677)

There comes a cry from all lands that prayer in the inner chamber
is, in general, neglected by those who call themselves believers.
Many make no use of it; they go to church and confess Christ,
but they know little of personal communion with God. Many
make little use of it except in a spirit of haste, and more as a matter of custom or for easing their conscience, [and] they cannot

tell of any joy or blessing in it …. Oh, what is it, then, that makes
the inner chamber so powerless? Is it not the deep sinfulness of
man and the dislike of his fallen nature for God that makes the
world and its fellowship more attractive than being alone with
the heavenly Father? Is it not that Christians do not believe the
word of God, which declares that the flesh that is in them is en-
mity against God (Rom. 8:7), and that they walk too much after
the flesh, so that the Spirit cannot strengthen them for prayer? [82]

~Andrew Murray (1828-1917)

*For those who live according to the flesh set their minds on
the things of the flesh, but those who live according to the
Spirit set their minds on the things of the Spirit …. [Don't]
live according to the flesh. For if you live according to the
flesh you will die, but if by the Spirit you put to death the
deeds of the body, you will live. (Rom. 8:5, 12-13)*

There is a swarm of hellish lusts as soldiers under the command
of the sin of our nature …. These wage war against the soul (1
Pet. 2:11). They seek to drive the soul from God …. Against these
also you must fight in faith, resist them, deny them, weaken,
mortify, and crucify them …. Make no provision for them, but
starve them, however painful that may be. "But put ye on the
Lord Jesus Christ, and make not provision for the flesh, to fulfill the lusts thereof" (Rom. 13:14). [83]

~Thomas Boston (1676-1732)

Guard vigilantly and strive prayerfully against that which creates a conscious distance between God and your soul. Is it the
world? — come out of it. Is it the *creature?* — relinquish it. Is it
the *flesh?* — mortify it. Is it *sin?* — forsake it. Is it *unbelief?* — nail
it to the cross. Oh, let nothing separate you from Christ — no
earthly good or carnal delight cause a distance, or coldness, or
shyness between God and your soul. Give Jesus your undivid-
ed heart, and let God be your all in all. [84]

~Octavius Winslow (1808-1878)

[O Lord], bid your Spirit to arise in all his might, and crush in-dwelling opponents! ... Strengthen us with heavenly aid in the inner man, lest we faint and be weary in the conflict—and yield to our bosom-foes. The enemy is within the citadel! Come with your almighty power and subdue him .... O Jesus, we are yours! Other lords have had dominion over us—but now we are your willing servants. Come, then, O you who are our Lord, pierce to the death—utterly destroy—abolish in us every par-ticle of carnal self! [85]

~Henry Law (1797-1884)

† † †

Forsake Worldliness

You must no longer walk as the Gentiles do, in the futility of their minds. † *Keep your heart with all vigilance, for from it flow the springs of life. (Eph. 4:17; Prov. 4:23)*

Keep the fountain of your heart clear all the day long, remem-bering that from it those holy affections (which in prayer you are to pour forth to God) must be drawn. [86]

~Richard Baxter (1615-1691)

The mind that is turned loose to wander after vanity [through-out] the day is unfit in an hour of prayer or meditation to be taken up with the love of God. It must be the work of the day, and of our lives, to walk in a fitness for [prayer], though we are not always in the immediate, lively exercise of it. [87]

~C.H. Spurgeon (1834-1892)

[For some], the world is first in the morning in their thoughts, and last at night, and almost all the day .... The world devours all the time almost that God and their souls should have: it will not give them leave to pray, or read, or meditate, or discourse of holy things. Even when they seem to be praying, or hearing the word of God, the world is in their thoughts. [88]

~C.H. Spurgeon (1834-1892)

Hours for the world! Moments for Christ! The world has our best and our prayer closet the remnants of our time. We give our strength and freshness to the ways of [wealth] and our fatigue to the ways of God. Therefore ... we need to be commanded to attend to that very act which it ought to be our greatest happiness, as it is our highest privilege to perform—to meet with our God! [89]

~Octavius Winslow (1808-1878)

[Some] indulge in amusements which I am sure are not consistent with prayer .... How can you come home from frivolity and sin, and then look into the face of Jesus? ... You cannot roll in the mire, and then approach with clean garments to the mercy seat! [90]

~William Gurnall (1616-1679)

What a fitness for prayer, for communion with God, for the reading of his sacred word, can a believer find ... in carnal song [and] in the immoral novel? What preparation of mind do these pursuits afford for approaching to God? [91]

~Richard Baxter (1615-1691)

As [Lot], that righteous man lived among them day after day, he was tormenting his righteous soul over their lawless deeds that he saw and heard. † What partnership has righteousness with lawlessness? Or what fellowship has light with darkness? ... Therefore go out from their midst, and be separate from them, says the Lord, and touch no unclean thing; then I will welcome you. † Let us also lay aside every weight, and sin which clings so closely, and let us run ... looking to Jesus. (2 Pet. 2:7-8; Heb. 12:1-2)

Mark well the places and society and companions that unhinge your hearts for communion with God and make your prayers drive heavily. There be on your guard. [92]

~*J.C. Ryle (1816-1900)*

The spirit of the world is the great hindrance to the spirit of prayer. All our most earnest calls to men to pray more will be vain except this evil be acknowledged and combated and overcome …. And how is this to be done? There is but one way—the cross of Christ, "by which," as Paul says, "the world is crucified unto me, and I unto the world" (Gal. 6:14). It is only through death to the world that we can be freed from its spirit. [93]

~*Andrew Murray (1828-1917)*

[Let] your dealings with this ungodly world be a constant battle …. It is utterly impossible that you can love the cross and love the world too. Faith in the cross, and confederacy with the enemies of the cross, are totally irreconcilable. We cannot carry Christ's cross upon our shoulder and the world in our hand at the same time. We cannot be truly crucified by the one and yet live to the other. [94]

~*Octavius Winslow (1808-1878)*

Whoever loves his life loses it, and whoever hates his life in this world will keep it for eternal life. † Do not love the world or the things in the world. If anyone loves the world, the love of the Father is not in him. (John 12:25; 1 John 2:15)

[Do you want to be more enabled] for prayer, and be frequent in it, and experience much of the pure sweetness of it? Then deny yourselves more the muddy pleasures and sweetness of the world. If you would pray much, and with much advantage, then be sober, and watch unto prayer. Suffer not your hearts to long after ease, and wealth, and esteem in the world. [95]

~*Robert Leighton (1611-1684)*

If you will be hotter in [prayer] you must be colder towards the world.... Wood that has the sap in it will not burn easily; neither will your heart readily take fire in holy duties [if you] come so sopped in the world to them. Drain, therefore, your heart of these eager affections.... [There is] no better way for this than to set your soul under the frequent meditation of Christ's love to you, your relation to him, with the great and glorious things you expect from him in another world. This, or nothing, will dry up your love to this world, as your wood which is laid a sunning is made fit for the fire. [96]

~William Gurnall (1616-1679)

[O Lord], cast out of my heart all worldliness.... May your love, O precious Savior, constrain me to surrender myself wholly to you ... that I who live may no longer live to myself, but unto you who died for us and rose again. (cf. 2 Cor. 5:14-15) [97]

~Edward Bickersteth (1786-1850)

[O Lord], deliver me from those excessive cares of this world, which would so engross my time and my thoughts, that the one thing needful should be forgotten .... May I never be too busy to attend to those great affairs which lie between you and my soul; never be so engrossed with the concerns of time, as to neglect the interests of eternity. [98]

~Philip Doddridge (1702-1751)

Two

Practical Steps Toward Prayer

✝ ✝ ✝

Prioritize Prayer as Indispensable

But seek first the kingdom of God and his righteousness. ✝ *Look carefully then how you walk ... making the best use of the time, because the days are evil. (Matt 6:33; Eph. 5:15-16)*

The greatest thing anyone can do for God and for man is to pray. It is not the only thing. But it is the chief thing. [1]

~*S.D. Gordon (1859-1936)*

You can do *more* than pray, *after* you have prayed. But you *cannot* do more than pray *until* you have prayed. [2]

~*S.D. Gordon (1859-1936)*

Time is a commodity of which there seems to be a universal and chronic shortage. Lack of time is a much overworked excuse for neglect of duty. And yet, strangely enough, even in the midst of exacting routine we always manage to find time for all we urgently want to do. In reality, the fundamental problem lies not in the *time factor*, but in the realm of *will* and *desire*. We each have all the time there is, and we each choose our own priorities. We automatically place first that which we consider most important. If prayer is meager, it is because we consider it supplemental, not fundamental. To our Lord it was not a reluctant addendum, but a fundamental necessity. The time we spend in prayer will depend on the way we allocate our priorities. If we share Christ's view of the indispensability of prayer, we will somehow make time for it. [3]

~J. Oswald Sanders (1902-1992)

Anything which hinders prayer must be wrong; if any management of the family, or lack of management, is injuring our power in prayer, there is an urgent demand for an alteration. [4]

~C.H. Spurgeon (1834-1892)

Prayers may be hindered ... by having too much to do .... The rich man in the parable had no time for prayer, for he was busy in planning new barns in which to bestow his goods—but he had to find time for dying when the Lord said, "This night shall your soul be required of you" (Luke 12:20). [5]

~C.H. Spurgeon (1834-1892)

Consider your ways .... You looked for much, and behold, it came to little. And when you brought it home, I blew it away. Why? declares the LORD of hosts. Because of my house that lies in ruins, while each of you busies himself with his own house. (Hag. 1:7-9)

We prove the value we attach to things by the time we devote to them. The Kingdom should be first every day, and all the day. Let the Kingdom be first every morning. Begin the day with God, and God himself will maintain his Kingdom in your heart. [6]

~Andrew Murray (1828-1917)

The perpetual hurry of business and company ruins me in soul if not in body. More solitude and earlier hours! I suspect I have been allotting habitually too little time to religious exercises ....

Hence, I am lean and cold and hard. I had better allot two hours or an hour and a half daily. I have been keeping too late hours, and hence have had but a hurried half hour in a morning to myself.[7]

~William Wilberforce (1759-1833)

Ah! how well might it have been with many a man, had he but spent one quarter of that time in closet prayer, that he has spent in curious inquiries after things that have not been fundamental to his happiness.[8]

~Thomas Brooks (1608-1680)

In this busy and engrossing world, when the mind is filled every morning with all the news of the ends of the earth, and the interest of the heart is held, as the eyes are held by a drama on the stage, God falls out of men's thoughts. If men will not sometimes think of God, he will become merely a name to them. If they glance toward him only now and again, and with an unobservant and undesiring eye, he will become strange and shadowy, and will remain unknown .... It is in prayer that we have the sure consciousness of God. Even though a man may kneel with a haze over his mind and a chill upon his spirit, he will not kneel in vain.[9]

~William M. Clow (1853-1930)

Most men lose their fervency and strength of their desires by misplacing them; they are zealous for such things as cannot ... pay them for their pains.[10]

~William Gurnall (1616-1679)

Oh pray! ... Rather neglect friends than not pray; rather fast and lose breakfast, dinner, tea, and supper—and sleep too—than not pray .... And we must not [merely] talk about prayer—we must pray in right earnest. The Lord is near. He comes softly while the virgins slumber.[11]

~Andrew Bonar (1810-1892)

Pursue hard after him. The Lord Christ sought you with bruises in his body and travail in his soul; and will you begrudge him an hour in duty, a little time in prayer? [12]

~*Thomas Manton (1620-1677)*

For the love of Christ controls us, because we have concluded this: that one has died for all, therefore all have died; and he died for all, that those who live might no longer live for themselves but for him who for their sake died and was raised. (2 Cor. 5:14-15)

Do you see this woman? ... She has wet my feet with her tears and wiped them with her hair .... She has not ceased to kiss my feet .... She has anointed my feet with ointment ... for she loved much. But he who is forgiven little, loves little. (Luke 7:44-47)

What men set their hearts upon, they will find time and place to effect it .... He who has an inflamed love to God will certainly find out a corner to enjoy secret communion with God. True lovers will find out corners to enjoy one another in. [13]

~*Thomas Brooks (1608-1680)*

Ah! friends, did you but love the Lord Jesus with a more strong, with a more raised love, you would never faint in [closet prayer] .... Divine love will make all closet duties easier to the soul, and more pleasant and delightful to the soul; and therefore, do all you can to strengthen your love to Christ. [14]

~*Thomas Brooks (1608-1680)*

Spirit of God, descend upon my heart,
Wean it from earth, through all its pulses move;
Stoop to my weakness, mighty as thou art,
And make me love thee as I ought to love. [15]

~*George Croly (1780-1860)*

✝ ✝ ✝

Prepare What to Pray For

Prepare your work outside; get everything ready for yourself in the field, and after that build your house. ✝ *O Lord, in the morning you hear my voice; in the morning I prepare a sacrifice for you and watch. (Prov. 24:27; Psa. 5:3)*

Lack of proper planning will be enough to make the prayer life of many unproductive and ineffective .... The labor of prayer requires a definite plan and purpose. I must know what work I have to do in my secret chamber before I enter into it.[16]

~O. Hallesby (1879-1961)

It is well to approach the seat of the King of kings as much as possible with premeditation and preparation, knowing what we are about, where we are standing, and what it is which we desire to obtain .... God forbid that our prayer should be a mere leaping out of one's bed and kneeling down, and saying anything that comes to hand; on the contrary, may we wait upon the Lord with holy fear and sacred awe.[17]

~C.H. Spurgeon (1834-1892)

The words of Scripture seem to encourage such a premeditation, when it tells us, we should "not be rash with our mouths, nor let our hearts be hasty to utter anything before God" (Ecc. 5:2).[18]

~Isaac Watts (1674-1748)

A most beneficial exercise in secret prayer before the Father is to write things down so that I see exactly what I think and want to say. Only those who have tried these ways know the ineffable benefit of such strenuous times in secret.[19]

~Oswald Chambers (1874-1917)

I find it well to preface prayer not only by meditation but by the definite request that I may be directed into the channels of prayer to which the Holy Spirit is beckoning me. I also find it helpful to make a short list, like notes prepared for a sermon, before every season of prayer. The mind needs to be guided as well as the spirit attuned. I can thus get my thoughts in order, and having prepared my prayer can put the notes on the table or chair before me, kneel down and get to business. [20]

~J.O. Fraser (1886-1938)

Do you not sometimes fall on your knees without thinking beforehand what you mean to ask God for? ... You will find it more helpful to your prayers, if you have some objectives at which you aim, and I think also, if you have some persons whom you will mention. Do not merely plead with God for sinners in general, but always mention some in particular. [21]

~C.H. Spurgeon (1834-1892)

Let your prayer be so specific that you can say as you go out, "I know what I have asked from my Father, and I expect an answer." It is a good plan sometimes to take a piece of paper and write down what you need to pray for. You might keep such a paper for a week or more, repeating the prayers until some new need arises. [22]

~Andrew Murray (1828-1917)

Intercession should be definite and detailed. Vagueness is lifelessness. Paul besought the Romans to pray for him, and then told them exactly what he wanted, four definite petitions to be presented for him (Rom. 15:30-32) .... It is considerable practical help if we make our intercession systematic, especially if the Lord gives us many to pray for. If every day has its written list of special names to be remembered, we shall be less likely to forget or drop them. Each several name was engraved on the breastplate of the high priest that it might be borne upon his heart continually. (Ex. 28:21, 29) [23]

~Frances R. Havergal (1836-1879)

A great reason why we reap so little benefit by prayer is because we rest too much in generals .... Besides, to be particular in our petitions would keep the spirit from wandering much when we are intent upon a weighty [request]. [24]

~Samuel Lee (1625-1691)

[It is essential in prayer] that some proper method be observed, not only that what is said be good, but that it be said in its proper place and time; and that we do not offer anything to the glorious Majesty of heaven and earth which is confused, [irreverent], and indigested. [25]

~Matthew Henry (1662-1714)

Cultivate that method of prayer which is most helpful, whether it be that of speaking aloud in loneliness, or of communing in stillness of heart and silence, whether standing or kneeling or sitting. No special [method] is insisted upon as necessary in the word of God. The matter of supreme importance is that we discover the method of prayer which helps us most actually to realize the presence of God and hold communion with him. The place, the time, the method, are matters concerning which there must be individual choice and decision. [26]

~G. Campbell Morgan (1863-1945)

As many as are the flowers of summer, so many are the varieties of prayer! But while prayers are of these various orders, there is one respect in which they are all one if they are acceptable with God—they must be, every one of them, in the Holy Spirit. [27]

~C.H. Spurgeon (1834-1892)

[O Lord], give us wisdom to discern what our own duties are, and grace in patient diligence and self-denial to fulfill them; and through all, may sweet intercourse in secret with our God be our hidden joy and consolation. [28]

~Edward Bickersteth (1786-1850)

† † †

Choose a Place for Prayer

But when you pray, go into your room and shut the door and pray to your Father who is in secret. And your Father who sees in secret will reward you. (Matt. 6:6)

In praying, the principal object to be sought, is to be alone with God. We should endeavor to find some place where no mortal eye sees us, and where we can pour out our hearts with the feeling that no one is looking at us but God …. When a person has a real desire to find some place where he can be in secret with his God, he will generally find a way.[29]

~J.C. Ryle (1816-1900)

Those who know how needful and helpful such secret times and places for prayer are, will secure, at any cost, the silent season even though, like the psalmist, it be found necessary to rise before others wake, and [precede] the dawning of the morning (Psa. 119:147). Yes, every praying soul needs to meet God absolutely alone. There are secrets of soul and spirit which no other human being however intimate ought to know, or indeed can know.[30]

~A.T. Pierson (1837-1911)

The greater measure any man has of the Spirit of God, the more that man will delight to be with God in secret …. The more any man has of the Spirit of Christ, the more he loves Christ, and the more any man loves Christ, the more he delights to be with Christ alone. Lovers love to be alone.[31]

~Thomas Brooks (1608-1680)

Do we not love God enough to make it an objective to shut ourselves in with him at times just to enjoy him?[32]

~A.T. Pierson (1837-1911)

Father, help me to pray; lead me into the quiet place.
When distractions pull away, bring me back and help me stay.[33]

~Anonymous

† † †

Set a Time for Prayer

*Look carefully then how you walk, not as unwise but as wise,
making the best use of the time, because the days are evil. Therefore
do not be foolish, but understand what the will of the Lord is.
(Eph. 5:15-17)*

Set up your resolutions, set your time, and keep your time. Do
not put off this duty by pretending you pray always …. "Get
you into your closet," says Christ; get a place [and] set a time
wherein you may make it your business to seek the Lord.[34]

~Richard Alleine (1610-1681)

Some people hinder their prayers … by a lack of order. They
get up a little too late, and they have to chase their work all the
day, and never overtake it. They are always in a flurry, one duty
tripping up the heels of another. They have no appointed time
for retirement, too little space hedged about for communion
with God, and consequently, something or other happens, and
prayer is forgotten.[35]

~C.H. Spurgeon (1834-1892)

[Others], give such undue attention to petty details that matters
of major importance are squeezed out. This is especially the
case where prayer is concerned.[36]

~J. Oswald Sanders (1902-1992)

It is vain to say, "I have too much work to do to find time." You must find time or forfeit blessing. God knows how to save for you the time you sacredly keep for communion with him. [37]

~Unknown

We [all] have been entrusted with the same amount of time, but not all use it in such a way that we produce a tenfold return …. We are not responsible for our capacity. We are responsible for the strategic investment of our time. If we consider prayer as a high priority, we will so arrange our day to make time for it. [38]

~J. Oswald Sanders (1902-1992)

It is not always possible for a will to find a way, but it is possible in the matter of prayer. Time *can* be found. One could begin with a minimum rule of fifteen minutes each day. Even so slight an investment of well-used time would bring a vast and precious gain. [39]

~William E. Sangster (1900-1960)

How many periods of five, ten, or fifteen minutes that could be devoted to prayer do we waste or leave unemployed in the course of a day? [40]

~J. Oswald Sanders (1902-1992)

It would revolutionize the lives of most men if they were shut in with God in some secret place for half an hour a day. [41]

~Samuel Chadwick (1860-1932)

A busy friend of mine spends three hours a day in prayer. Let no one be intimidated by that …. Fifteen minutes in the morning and ten at night, consistently adhered to, would begin to make amazing differences in the life of any man or woman. [42]

~William E. Sangster (1900-1960)

There is no rule in Scripture as to how often you should pray, and there is no rule as to when you should pray; it is left to the man's own gracious spirit to suggest seasons. We do not need to go back to the bondage of the Mosaic covenant, to be under rule and rubric; we are left to that free Spirit who leads his saints aright. Yet, three times a day is a commendable number. [43]

~C.H. Spurgeon (1834-1892)

Evening and morning and at noon I utter my complaint and moan, and he hears my voice. † *[Daniel] went to his house where he had windows in his upper chamber open toward Jerusalem. He got down on his knees three times a day and prayed and gave thanks before his God, as he had done previously. (Psa. 55:17; Dan. 6:10)*

It is good to have our hours of prayer, not to *bind*, but to *remind* conscience. [44]

~Matthew Henry (1662-1714)

Consecrate such a part of time as will suit with your occasions, your course of life, according to your abilities and opportunities. It is an expression of love to God to give him [something] that is your own; and it will be of exceeding profit to you. [45]

~Thomas Manton (1620-1677)

To effect a radical change in our use of time so as to make more time for prayer will require strength of purpose and a deep dependence on the Lord's enabling. [46]

~J. Oswald Sanders (1902-1992)

[O Lord], strengthen our resolutions, and give us your grace to carry them [out] patiently and steadily. [47]

~Edward Bickersteth (1786-1850)

† † †

Stick to the Appointed Time

The end of all things is at hand; therefore, be self-controlled and sober-minded for the sake of your prayers. (1 Pet. 4:7)

[Do you] hear Satan and your flesh whispering in your ear ....
"This is not a fit time for praying. Stay for a more convenient
season." ... Now beware, Christian, your foot is near a snare ....
When the flesh or Satan beg time of you, it is to steal time from
you. They [delay you] at one time, on a design to shut you out
at last from this duty at any time.[48]

~William Gurnall (1616-1679)

Certainly, if we are to have a quiet hour set down in the midst
of a hurry of duties, and kept [invariably], we must exercise
both forethought and self-denial. We must be prepared to forgo
many things that are pleasant, and some things that are profitable. We shall have to redeem the time.[49]

~David McIntyre (1859-1938)

Oh, if you did but know what you are made for and your high
destiny, you would not waste your time in the [trivial] things
that occupy your hands and your souls! ... God forgive those
moments of frivolity which ought to have been occupied in
prayer![50]

~C.H. Spurgeon (1834-1892)

One thing you must learn to do. Whatever you leave undone,
you must not leave this undone .... You must force yourself
to be alone and to pray. Do make a point of this .... You will
easily find excuses. Work is so pressing, and work is necessary.
Other engagements take time. You are tired. You want to go to
bed. You go to bed late and want to get up late. So simple prayer
and devotion are crowded out. And yet ... the necessity is par-

amount [and inescapable]. If you and I are ever to be of any good, if we are to be a blessing, not a curse, to those with whom we are connected ... we must be alone with the only Source of unselfishness. [51]

~Forbes Robinson (1867-1904)

[You may say], "I can't pray when I don't feel like it." Yes, you can. You can say to your Lord, "Lord Jesus, I don't feel like speaking to You. I'm sorry about that. Why is it so?" ... Never mind your feelings. The one thing that matters is not to stay away from your Lord because of them. Tell him that your feelings are all wrong and ask him to put you right. [52]

~Amy Carmichael (1867-1951)

[Some] assume that prayers are only efficacious when they rise forth from an eager and emotional heart. Nothing could be further from the truth .... We must keep our appointments with God, whether we feel like it or not .... God can do more for us when we pray against inclination than when we pray with it. The meek submission of our will deepens our surrender, [and] our resolution to engage in prayer strengthens thought control. We rise from such prayers infinitely stronger than if we had knelt only at the dictate of desire. Faith, not feeling, measures the efficacy of prayer. [53]

~William E. Sangster (1900-1960)

I will not slacken my seeking the face of God, though now, when I try to pray, I am so full of darkness, horror, and confusion, that I am not able to pray as formerly. Yet when I can't pray, I'll groan. [54]

~Cotton Mather (1663-1728)

Whatever your position, if you cannot speak, cry; if you cannot cry, groan. If you cannot groan, let there be "groans which cannot be uttered." And if you cannot even rise to that point, let your prayer be at least a breathing—a vital, sincere desire—the outpouring of your inner life in the simplest and weakest form, and God will accept it. [55]

~*C.H. Spurgeon (1834-1892)*

Not to pray because you do not feel fit to pray is like saying, "I will not take medicine because I am too ill." Pray for prayer! Pray yourself, by the Spirit's assistance, into a praying frame! ... So, under a sense of prayerlessness, be more intent on prayer. Repent that you cannot repent, groan that you cannot groan and pray until you do pray—in so doing *God will help you.* [56]

~*C.H. Spurgeon (1834-1892)*

When you can pray and long to pray—why, then, you *will* pray! But when you cannot pray and do not wish to pray—why, then, you *must* pray, or evil will come of it! He is on the brink of ruin who forgets the Mercy Seat! [57]

~*C.H. Spurgeon (1834-1892)*

Beware of the first beginnings of a neglect [of secret prayer]. Watch against temptations to it. Take heed how you begin to allow of excuses. Be watchful to keep up the duty in the height of it; let it not so much as begin to sink. For when you give way, though it be but a little, it is like giving way to an enemy in the field of battle; the first beginning of a retreat greatly encourages the enemy and weakens the retreating soldiers. [58]

~*Jonathan Edwards (1703-1758)*

For a long time, indeed for years, I can see that [Satan] has contrived very many days to prevent my praying to any purpose. His temptations to me lie in the direction of putting half-lawful literature or literary work before me, which I am led on to read at once, without having first of all fully met with God. In short, [Satan] succeeds in reversing in my case, 'Seek first the kingdom of God.' Lord, give me power to resist, [and] from this day give me many victories where formerly I fell under him. [59]

~*Andrew Bonar (1810-1892)*

Be faithful in the inner chamber, [and] thank him that you can count on him to meet you there. Although everything appears cold, dark, and strained, bow in silence before the loving Lord Jesus, who desires you to commune with him, [and] thank the Father that he has given you the Spirit. [60]

~Andrew Murray (1828-1917)

[O Lord], enable us to perceive and be assured that prayer unto you is our richest privilege and our greatest honor. We do indeed mourn before you that most sad and affecting proof of our depravity, that we are so backward to this blessed duty, and so soon weary of it …. Our spirit so soon flags and our thoughts so soon wander. We are so reluctant to commence and so ready to give up prayer unto you. [But we thank you for] the happy times, when we realize our true honor, privilege, and blessedness in communion with you! Oh, that this day we may find it good to draw near unto you. [61]

~Edward Bickersteth (1786-1850)

† † †

Confront Laziness and Lethargy

Do not be slothful in zeal …. Be constant in prayer. (Rom. 12:11-12)

Let us ever be on our guard against the slothful, indolent, lazy spirit in religion, which is natural to us all, and especially in the matter of our private prayers. When we feel that spirit creeping over us, let us remember Peter, James, and John in the garden, and take care. [62]

~J.C. Ryle (1816-1900)

Sleep not away your time for prayer in the morning, and then think you are sufficiently excused for omitting it because your worldly business calls you another way. Jade not your body with over-laboring, nor overcharge your mind with too heavy a load of worldly cares in the day, and then think that the weariness of the one, and discomposure of the other, will discharge you from praying again at night.[63]

~William Gurnall (1616-1679)

Zeal and diligence take the opportunity, which sloth and negligence let slip. They are up with the sun, and "work while it is day;" they "seek the LORD while he may be found, and call upon him while he is near."[64]

~Richard Baxter (1615-1691)

God deserves [that] the prime and strength of your soul should be bestowed on him in your prayers. He gave you the powers of your soul and all your affections. Therefore, when you are going to pray, call up your affections, which by chance are asleep, … "What [are you doing], O sleeper? Arise, call upon your God."[65]

~William Gurnall (1616-1679)

We should stir up ourselves to lay hold on him; we should rouse mind and heart, graces and affections, that all may be stirring and active, and not shut up in a careless, drowsy listlessness. This is to watch unto prayer; this is to be vigilant and careful about it.[66]

~David Clarkson (1622-1686)

David says, "Why art thou cast down, O my soul? Awake psaltery and harp, I myself will awake early: my soul wait thou upon God" (Psa. 42:11; 108:2; 62:5). Nothing is more common in the Psalms than such interruptions and diversions from the immediate exercise, to raise up the heart to a higher tune in prayer and [in] praises. And this may be exceptionally useful, for [with] such heart reasonings and debates a saint may wind up his spirit and make himself better prepared.[67]

~Oliver Heywood (1630-1702)

It is no easy thing to pray and to work a lazy, dead heart into a necessary height of affection. The weights in a clock always run downward, but they are wound up by force, "To you, O LORD, I lift up my soul" (Psa. 25:1).[68]

~*Thomas Manton (1620-1677)*

Some may be ready to say they cannot be earnest. They oftentimes find themselves dull and spiritless, that they have not their hearts in [their prayers]. But when it is so ... you should be earnest in wrestling with a dull and hard heart.[69]

~*Jonathan Edwards (1703-1758)*

He that would have the kingdom of heaven must use violence to take it (cf. Matt. 11:12) .... He must use *violence* in his prayers, ... that is, he must wrestle and strive in them, and be fervent in them .... Therefore stir up yourselves, and consider what it will cost you.[70]

~*John Preston (1587-1628)*

Jacob said, "I will not let you go unless you bless me." †
In his manhood [Jacob] strove with God. He strove with the angel and prevailed; he wept and sought his favor. †
Therefore lift your drooping hands and strengthen your weak knees. (Gen. 32:26; Hos. 12:3-4; Heb. 12:12)

Awake, cold lips, and sing! Arise, dull knees, and pray;
Lift up, O man, your heart and eyes; Brush slothfulness away.
....
Cast every weight aside! Do battle with each sin;
Fight with the faithless world without, the faithless heart within.[71]

~*Horatius Bonar (1808-1889)*

Surely when a duty [like secret prayer] is lined with difficulty, and your corrupt heart draws back, having a great reluctance to do it, ... God intends to give you [extraordinary help] by it. Therefore, do not say a word against it, but stir yourself up, spur your heart onward; shake off sloth and run to God no matter what Satan, the world, or the flesh may say to the contrary.[72]

~*Oliver Heywood (1630-1702)*

When things are dying and fainting in the soul, we are to strengthen ourselves ... [and] chide the heart for its deadness in [prayer] .... And after you have done this, then look up, and expect this grace from God in and through Christ Jesus, [for he] said, "I am come that they may have life, and have it more abundantly" (John 10:10).[73]

~*Thomas Manton (1620-1677)*

[O Lord], strengthen us where we are weak, and [make us] feel our entire weakness and insufficiency that we may be ever looking to you for grace and strength.[74]

~*Edward Bickersteth (1786-1850)*

[O Lord], as frail creatures, we need grace and strength continually .... We are here before you, needy and destitute, bringing as it were our empty vessels. Lord, give us the water of life [and] replenish us from the fullness which is in Christ Jesus.[75]

~*Samuel Knight (1759–1827)*

† † †

Meditate on Truth

Give ear to my words, O LORD, consider my meditation. †
As I mused, the fire burned; then I spoke with my tongue.
(Psa. 5:1 KJV; 39:3)

Desires blown by meditation are the sparks that set prayer alight in flame.[76]

~*Samuel Lee (1625-1691)*

Meditation before prayer is like the tuning of an instrument and setting it for harmony …. The great reason our prayers are ineffectual, is because we do not meditate before them. [77]

~William Bates (1625-1699)

The Christian is like some heavy birds, as the bustard and others, that cannot get upon the wing without a run …. Now, meditation is the great instrument you are to use in this preparatory work. [78]

~William Gurnall (1616-1679)

Meditation is the best beginning of prayer, and prayer is the best conclusion of meditation. When the Christian, like Daniel, has first opened the windows of his soul by contemplation, then he may kneel down to pray. [79]

~George Swinnock (1627-1673)

Meditation on our sins helps in confession, meditation on our [needs] helps in petition, meditation on our mercies helps in thanksgiving. A Christian ought to keep a catalogue, at least in the table-book of his heart, of these three particulars. David did so; he [recalled] his unrighteousness, or the wrong he had done to God, "My sin is ever before me" (Psa. 51:3). He thought much upon his [needs] and sufferings, he often cried out, … "My sorrow is ever before me" (Psa. 38:17). And for God's mercies, he did not write them in the sand, but he treasured them up in his memory. "Thy lovingkindness is before mine eyes" (Psa. 26:3). [80]

~George Swinnock (1627-1673)

I believe it is the experience of many who love secret devotion that at times they cannot pray, for their heart seems hard, cold, dumb, and almost dead. Do not pump up unwilling and formal prayer, my brethren; but take down the hymn-book and sing. While you praise the Lord for what you have, you will find your rocky heart begin to dissolve and flow in rivers. [81]

~C.H. Spurgeon (1834-1892)

Do you ever find prayer difficult because of tiredness or dryness? When that is so, it is an immense help to let the psalms and hymns we know by heart say themselves or sing themselves inside of us .... Hymns, little prayer-songs of our own, even the simplest of them, can sing us into ... the consciousness of his love, for we are never for one moment out of it. [82]

~Amy Carmichael (1867-1951)

Have you ever felt discouraged in prayer because words would not come? Often our Lord Jesus turned Bible words into prayer. The Psalm book was the prayer book of the early Church. It is ours still. We cannot ever fathom the depths of this book .... Is there a need it cannot meet? Is there a dryness it cannot refresh? [83]

~Amy Carmichael (1867-1951)

The first thing the child of God has to do morning by morning is to obtain food for his inner man .... Now what is the food for the inner man? Not prayer, but the word of God; and here again not the simple reading of the word of God, so that it only passes through our minds, just as water runs through a pipe, but considering what we read, pondering over it, and applying it to our hearts. [84]

~George Müller (1805-1898)

[O Lord], give us an increasing love of your holy word. [Prompt] and incline us to read it more frequently, to meditate upon it more seriously, and to pray over it more fervently. [85]

~Samuel Knight (1759–1827)

The reading of the Scriptures ... is a part of our daily work, and should ordinarily accompany our prayers and praises. When we speak to God, we must hear what God says to us, and thus the communion is complete. [86]

~Matthew Henry (1662-1714)

To keep up a good fire of zeal, we must have much fuel …. If I understand aright, zeal is the fruit of the Holy Spirit, and genuine zeal draws its life and vital force from the continued operations of the Holy Spirit in the soul. Next to this, zeal feeds upon truths. [87]

~C.H. Spurgeon (1834-1892)

Read the Holy Scriptures, and such lively writings as help you to understand and practice them. As going to the fire is our way when we are cold, to cure our numbness, so reading over some part of a warm and quickening book, will do much to warm and quicken a benumbed soul: and it is [a great] help to rouse us up to prayer or meditation, and put life into us before we address ourselves more nearly unto God. I have found it myself a great help. [88]

~Richard Baxter (1615-1691)

It is advisable to use the Bible especially and afterwards some spirit-stirring book, be it memoir or spiritual treatise, to stir up the black hot coals and compel them to break into a heaven-ascending flame. [89]

~F.B. Meyer (1847-1929)

[But beware]; reading one hundred expositions *about* prayer will never equal one vital experience *of* prayer. [90]

~Leonard Ravenhill (1907-1994)

One acorn begets one oak, … [and] just one seed-thought gathered from the word of God may "spark a man off" in prayer for hours. [91]

~Leonard Ravenhill (1907-1994)

O Lord, our souls do indeed cleave to the dust (Psa. 119:25). They ought to soar upwards, and live as in your presence; but we find by sad and humbling experience, that they are perpetually groveling here below, filled with the cares of this life, the deceitfulness of riches, and the [desires for] other things (Mark 4:19). Quicken us according to your word; … quicken us according to your command to love you with all our heart and mind and soul and strength; quicken us according to the sureness and fullness of your promises. [92]

~*Edward Bickersteth (1786-1850)*

† † †

Do It! Do it! Do it!

But be doers of the word, and not hearers only, deceiving yourselves…. [Not a] hearer who forgets but a doer who acts, he will be blessed in his doing. (Jam. 1:22-25)

It is one of the greatest dangers in religion that we rest content with the pleasure and approval which a beautiful representation of a truth calls forth, without the immediate performance of what it demands. It is only when conviction has been translated into conduct that we have proof that the truth is mastering us. [93]

~*Andrew Murray (1828-1917)*

The main lesson about prayer is just this: Do it! Do it! Do it! You want to be taught to pray. My answer is: pray and never faint, and then you shall never fail. [94]

~*John Laidlow (1832-1906)*

Everyone then who hears these words of mine and does them will be like a wise man who built his house on the rock. † If you know these things, blessed are you if you do them. (Matt. 7:24; John 13:17)

We do not know much about prayer, but surely this need not prevent us from praying! We do know what our Lord has taught us about prayer. And we do know that he has sent the Holy Spirit to teach us all things. (John 14:26)[95]

~Albert Richardson (1868-19__)

It is useless to say you know not how to pray .... It is simply speaking to God. It needs neither learning nor wisdom nor book-knowledge to begin it .... The weakest infant can cry when he is hungry. The poorest beggar can hold out his hand for alms, and does not wait to find fine words.[96]

~J.C. Ryle (1816-1900)

This is the only way we shall ever learn to pray, *by just beginning to do it.* And as the babbling child learns the art of speech by speaking, and the lark mounts up to the heights of the sky by beating its little wings again and again upon the air, so [in prayer, God] will teach us how to pray; and the more we pray, the more shall we learn the mysteries and heights and depths of prayer.[97]

~A.B. Simpson (1843-1919)

The Father takes it kindly when the child is striving to obey him, though it may fall very far short. He sees that the spirit is willing, though the flesh is weak, and accepts our upright attempts.[98]

~Oliver Heywood (1630-1702)

[Consider] the great delight the Lord takes in pure obedience. "To obey is better than sacrifice." (1 Sam. 15:22) ... To pray in pure obedience is to set upon the duty when there is no assistance visible or encouragement sensible .... Thus, when a soul, after a faithful use of means, finds his heart dead and dull, yet in obedience to the command kneels down—though the sense of his inability is so great that he questions whether he shall have power to speak one word to God as he ought, ... he may hope to meet God [on] his way.[99]

~William Gurnall (1616-1679)

[Lord], let your hand be ready to help me, for I have chosen your precepts. (Psa.119:173)

Lord, you command me to pray. I cannot pray as I would—yet
I will obey; for though [I think] my prayer is not acceptable—
yet your own commandment is acceptable to you. [100]

~*Martin Luther (1483-1546)*

O friends! take heed of dallying, delaying, trifling, and going
about the bush, when you should be falling upon the work of
prayer .... Do as well as you can, and you shall find acceptance
with God: For if there be first a willing mind, it is accepted according to what a man has, and not according to what he does
not have. (2 Cor. 8:12) [101]

~*Thomas Brooks (1608-1680)*

Begin by giving at least ten minutes a day definitely to this work.
It is in *doing* that we learn to *do*; it is as we take hold and begin
that the help of God's Spirit will come. It is as we daily hear
God's call, and at once put it into practice, that the consciousness [of his presence] will begin to live in us. [102]

~*Andrew Murray (1828-1917)*

Nothing would be better for most of us than a great revival in
our habits of private prayer. Perhaps we cannot do as Luther,
who was accustomed to say, "I have so much work to do today
that I cannot get through it with less than three hours of prayer."
... But that we should pray *more*, that we should *labor* in prayer
as Epaphras did, that we should *cultivate* the art of prayer is
clear. Habits of prayer need careful cultivation. The instinct and
impulse are with us by the grace of the Holy Spirit, but we need
to cultivate the gracious inward movements until they become
solidified into an unbending practice. [103]

~*F.B. Meyer (1847-1929)*

Prayer is a fine delicate instrument .... However, certain re-
quirements must also be met if the art of prayer is to be acquired
... *practice* and *perseverance*. Without practice no Christian will

become a real man or woman of prayer. And practice cannot be attained without perseverance. [104]

~*O. Hallesby (1879-1961)*

Come now, … turn aside for a while from your daily employment; escape for a moment from the tumult of your thoughts. Put aside your weighty cares; let your burdensome distractions wait. Free yourself a while for God and rest a while in him. Enter the inner chamber of your soul; shut out everything except God and that which can help you in seeking him, and when you have shut the door, seek him. Now, my whole heart, say to God, … "LORD, it is your face I seek" (Psa. 27:8).[105]

~*Anselm of Canterbury (c. 1033-1109)*

Three

Steps during Prayer

† † †

Ask for Help

Apart from me you can do nothing. (John 15:5)

When you are seeking to excite or exercise any grace, send up a fervent request to God to show his love and power upon your dead and sluggish heart. [1]

~*Richard Baxter (1615-1691)*

We cannot, without the Spirit's assistance, bring our hearts into a right frame for prayer. Our inability to do so is the reason why [prayer seems so awkward]. [2]

~*Thomas Ridgley (1667-1734)*

Pray by the Spirit's assistance; seek it, wait for it; do nothing that may check or restrain it, and give any impediment to it. Rely not upon inward abilities, or outward helps, real or pretended, so as to disengage that blessed Spirit …. Depend upon him alone who can help you to make requests in everything. [3]

~*David Clarkson (1622-1686)*

Be earnest with God in prayer to move and order your heart in its thoughts and desires …. It is not in man, not in the holiest on earth, to do this without divine assistance. Therefore, we find David so often crying out in this respect to order his steps in his word, to unite his heart to his fear, to incline his heart to his testimonies. (Psa. 119:133, 86:11, 119:36) [4]

~William Gurnall (1616-1679)

[When] looking upon the multitude of temptations without, and of corruptions within himself, and the weakness of the grace he has, [a Christian might say], "Alas! How can this be? Shall I ever attain my journey's end?" But again, when he looks upward and lifts his eyes above his difficulties, behold, the strength of God [is] engaged for him [and] directs his prayers. [5]

~Robert Leighton (1611-1684)

God is always ready to give us his grace; all he requires is that we should ask for it. Let us pray then and form habits of prayer, and God will give us grace abundantly. [6]

~Phillips Brooks (1835-1893)

Supposing your state is the worst that can be, your frame of mind the most unfavorable, your cross the heaviest, your corruption the strongest, your heart the hardest; still go to the throne of grace, and opening your case to the Lord with groanings that cannot be uttered, you shall adopt the song of David, who could say in the worst state, and in most pressing times, "But I give myself unto prayer" (Psa. 109:4). [7]

~Octavius Winslow (1808-1878)

Do not stay away from the throne of grace because of an unfavorable state of mind …. Do not yield then to this device of your adversary to keep you from prayer. It is the privilege of a poor soul to go to Jesus at his worst, to go in darkness, to go in weak faith, to go when everything says "stay away," to go in the face of opposition, to hope against hope, to go in the consciousness of having walked at a distance, to press through the crowd to the throne of grace, to take the hard, the cold, the reluctant heart and lay it before the Lord. O what a triumph this is of the power and the grace of the blessed Spirit in a poor believer! [8]

~Octavius Winslow (1808-1878)

Heavenly Father, by your Holy Spirit, help us now to pray. We feel our weakness, our ignorance, our deep corruptions …. We know that we have no power of ourselves, to keep ourselves. Our best strength, is utter weakness. Our firmest resolves, are as fleeting as the morning cloud and early dew. Oh! then never leave us nor forsake us. [9]

~Henry Law (1797-1884)

✝ ✝ ✝

Acknowledge God's Presence

Be still, and know that I am God. ✝ *Be not rash with your mouth, nor let your heart be hasty to utter a word before God, for God is in heaven and you are on earth. (Psa. 46:10; Ecc. 5:2)*

Don't rush into God's presence as though it were a common thing. We have a God who notices the preparation of the heart. [10]

~Philip Doddridge (1702-1751)

Let us take a few moments before we enter upon such solemnities, to pause and reflect on the perfections of the God we are addressing [and] on the importance of the business we are about to engage in …. When engaged, let us maintain a strict watchfulness over our own spirits, and check the first wanderings of thought. [11]

~Amy Carmichael (1867-1951)

The first rule of right prayer is to have our heart and mind framed as becomes those who are entering into conversation with God. [12]

~*John Calvin (1509-1564)*

[The tempter] would keep you in a lazy, sluggish coldness, to read, and hear, and pray as asleep, as if you did it not. Awake yourselves with the presence of God, and the great concernment of what you are about [to do]. [13]

~*Richard Baxter (1615-1691)*

[When we pray], it is most fitting for us first to feel that we are doing something that is *real*; that we are about to address ourselves to God, whom we cannot see, but who is *really present*. [14]

~*C.H. Spurgeon (1834-1892)*

It is the realization of that second Person as *really present*, the consciousness of the divine presence, which makes prayer real. [15]

~*C.H. Spurgeon (1834-1892)*

When you go to private prayer your first thought must be: *the Father is in secret; the Father awaits me there.* [16]

~*Andrew Murray (1828-1917)*

Let this be your chief object in prayer, to realize the presence of your heavenly Father. [17]

~*Andrew Murray (1828-1917)*

I find it helpful to begin [prayer] ... in adoring love and wonder of [God's] character and attributes, of his majesty and might, of his grace and glory. Musing kindles the fire, and the flame becomes "a wall of fire round about," which keeps beasts and intruders at a safe distance. [18]

~*Samuel Chadwick (1860-1932)*

O the vainness of our hearts! And how hard is it to establish them on him who dwells on high! Even while we are speaking to him, we suffer them to break loose and rove, and to entertain foolish thoughts. We would not [treat] a king or great person so, nor any man whom we respect, when we are speaking to him seriously. [19]

~Anthony Burgess (1600-1663)

If the majesty of an earthly king strikes such terror, then ought not the presence of so great a God? ... How can distraction and divisions enter into your heart when it is applying itself to such infinite greatness? [20]

~Robert Leighton (1611-1684)

How is it possible to keep the world from coming in and the mind from straying out? ... Let [our] first act be to affirm the fact of the holy Presence. Call every faculty of mind and body to remembrance, recognition, and realization of the God that is in secret and sees in secret. Hold the mind to this fact. Tolerate no distraction, allow no diversion, indulge no [amusement]. [21]

~Samuel Chadwick (1860-1932)

[Beware of the] danger of substituting [a form of] prayer and Bible study for living fellowship with God .... Your Bible study may so interest you, and so waken pleasing religious sentiment, that [even] the very word of God may become a substitute for God himself, [and hinder your] fellowship because it keeps the soul occupied instead of leading it to God. [22]

~Andrew Murray (1828-1917)

Rest not content with the form of prayer, the duty of prayer, the act of prayer. Be not satisfied unless [you are] conscious of the listening ear of God, the responding heart of Jesus, the vital breathing of the Spirit. Oh, let your communion with heaven be a blessed reality. Do not leave the Mercy-Seat without some evidence that you have been in solemn, holy, precious audience with the Invisible One .... Leave it not until God in Christ has spoken to you face to face. [23]

~Octavius Winslow (1808-1878)

We should never leave our prayer closets in the morning, without having concentrated our thoughts deeply and intensely on the fact of the actual presence of God: there with us, encompassing us, and filling the room as literally as it fills heaven itself. [24]

~F.B. Meyer (1847-1929)

Be not satisfied to think slightly and superficially of God. Take time to consider him, and know who he is; and then you will reverence him in your thoughts .... Shall we shut out God, or think any sudden passing look enough for him? [25]

~Robert Leighton (1611-1684)

The Lord is in his holy temple; let all the earth keep silence before him. † *[Mary] sat at the Lord's feet and listened to his teaching.* (Hab. 2:20; Luke 10:39)

[O Lord], make it our chief joy—to study you, to meditate on you, to gaze on you, to hold communion with you! ... May we be like Mary, sitting meekly at your feet. [26]

~Henry Law (1797-1884)

Enable me, O God, to collect and compose my thoughts before an immediate approach to you in prayer. May I be careful to have my mind in order when I take upon myself the honor to speak to the sovereign Lord of the universe .... You are infinitely too great to be trifled with, too wise to be imposed on by a mock devotion, and abhor a sacrifice without a heart. Help me to entertain a habitual sense of your perfections as an admirable help against cold and formal performances. Save me from engaging in rash and precipitate prayers, and from abrupt breaking away to follow business or pleasure as though I had never prayed. [27]

~Susanna Wesley (1669-1742)

† † †

Express your Needs and Desires

Do not be anxious about anything, but in everything by prayer and supplication with thanksgiving let your requests be made known to God. † Let us then with confidence draw near to the throne of grace, that we may receive mercy and find grace to help in time of need.
(Phil. 4:6; Heb. 4:16)

There are two things which will [always] bring the Christian to the throne of grace: a sense of his own [needs] and a desire to enjoy the presence of God. [28]

~Edward Bickersteth (1786-1850)

"He has filled the hungry with good things; and the rich he has sent empty away" (Luke 1:53) .... They that do not feel their need of [God's] blessing will soon sit down easy without it, ... but a pinching sense of need is necessary to excite the soul. [29]

~Thomas Boston (1676-1732)

Those that are most pinched with [their] sense of need, will readily come [with] best speed [to] the throne of grace. [30]

~Thomas Boston (1676-1732)

[Real prayer] is forced out of you by the overwhelming sense of your need. [31]

~C.H. Spurgeon (1834-1892)

As the needy only will stoop to ask for alms, so a real, deep, and abiding sense of our [poverty] is the first spring of a true and earnest desire to obtain help from God. [32]

~Edward Bickersteth (1786-1850)

[The nature of prayer] lies precisely in offering up our desires to God for things that we need. It is ... a pouring out [of] our

heart before the Lord (Psa. 62:8), a lifting [up of] our soul to him
(Psa. 25:1), a presenting [of] our supplications to him. (Dan. 9:18)[33]

~*Thomas Boston (1676-1732)*

Prayer and supplication, mingled with the fragrance of thanksgiving, must tell out the story of need and desire into the ear of the
Great Father. Spread the letter before him .... Just tell him how
things are with you, what you hoped, [and] what you want.[34]

~ *F.B. Meyer (1847-1929)*

[Let us then] express all our [needs] to our God with the utmost
plainness and simplicity as David did, when he could say, "I
poured out my complaint before him, [I told] before him my
trouble" (Psa. 142:2). No art is needed; no extraordinary talent
required [in this].[35]

~*Edward Bickersteth (1786-1850)*

"Let us draw nigh to God with a true heart" (Heb. 10:22) .... God
looks not so much to the elegance of your prayers, how *neat*
they are, nor to the [fullness] of your prayers, how *long* they
are, but to the sincerity of your prayers, how *hearty* they are.[36]

~*George Swinnock (1627-1673)*

[O God], let not our prayers be mere lifeless words, but the very
wishes of our hearts.[37]

~*Edward Bickersteth (1786-1850)*

[Let us] open our hearts unto him .... What the heart feels, the
mouth will express .... Dwell, therefore, chiefly on those things
which the Bible shows you to be of the greatest [importance]
and with which you are most deeply affected; which are warm-
est in your own hearts.[38]

~*Edward Bickersteth (1786-1850)*

Let us learn thus to plead the precepts, the promises, and whatever else may serve [us], but let us always have something to
plead, ... for pleading is the very marrow of prayer.[39]

~C.H. Spurgeon (1834-1892)

[Let us] go with our whole soul to God .... Shall God be expected to give to us that which we do not value? ... Are we to
treat him as though it were quite enough for him if we gave him
a stray thought or a half-hearted desire now and then?[40]

~C.H. Spurgeon (1834-1892)

Open your mouth wide, and I will fill it. (Psa. 81:10)

Believe that Jesus has the Spirit of grace and supplication for
you; look to him and he will, by his grace, help you to be both
sincere and fervent in your prayers.[41]

~Edward Bickersteth (1786-1850)

[O Lord], may the Spirit of grace and supplication ever breathe
in our earnest breathings. Strengthen us with lively assurance
that faithful prayer in Jesus' name grasps the arm of your om-
nipotence, achieves wonders [and] obtains blessings.[42]

~Henry Law (1797-1884)

[O Lord], prepare us now to come before you in prayer. Give us
... a spirit of fervent and enlarged desire for your grace, according to your own most gracious promise, "Open your mouth
wide, and I will fill it."[43]

~Edward Bickersteth (1786-1850)

† † †

Offer to God Thanksgiving

... in everything by prayer and supplication with thanksgiving †
Offer to God a sacrifice of thanksgiving, and perform your vows to
the Most High, and call upon me in the day of trouble; I will deliver
you, and you shall glorify me. (Phil. 4:6; Psa. 50:14-15)

[Thanksgiving is] a necessary ingredient in all our prayers ....
This spice must be in all our offerings. He that prays for [the]
mercy he wants, and is not thankful for mercies received, may
seem mindful of himself, but he is forgetful of God. [44]

~William Gurnall (1616-1679)

Can it be right to think only of ourselves, to pray for benefits and never honor our Benefactor? ... God forbid that we
should fall into a spirit so [base] and narrow. Healthy praise and
thanksgiving must be cultivated, because they prevent prayer
from becoming overgrown with the mildew of selfishness. [45]

~C.H. Spurgeon (1834-1892)

Our causes for [giving thanks] are innumerable. We are to be
thankful—that we have a prayer-hearing God to go to; that we
have wide and free access to his throne; that we are upon praying ground, not in the regions of despair; that we have got so
many answers to prayer; that we have obtained so many blessings unasked; that everything we need we may ask for. What
thankfulness should fill us! [46]

~Horatius Bonar (1808-1889)

Bless the LORD, O my soul, and forget not all his benefits,
who forgives all your iniquity, who heals all your diseases,
who redeems your life from the pit, who crowns you with
steadfast love and mercy, who satisfies you with good so
that your youth is renewed like the eagle's. (Psa. 103:2-5)

[A life] spent in prayer, amid the practical things of every day, will have as many divine causes for thanksgiving as it has for supplication. Everything that comes to us will be a new testimony to the goodness and faithfulness of God, ... [leading us to] sing evermore, "I will bless the Lord at all times; his praise shall continually be in my mouth" (Psa. 34:1). [47]

~A.B. Simpson (1843-1919)

What are our lives—but testimonies to divine faithfulness? We look back with gratitude and thankfulness on a wondrous past— the innumerable mercies which have been showered upon us ... in the midst of our ingratitude and sin. Bless the Lord, O our souls, and forget not all his benefits! Where would we now [be], but for [God's] great love to us in Christ! [48]

~John MacDuff (1818-1895)

[O Lord], we are lost in wonder ... when we reflect upon your goodness and mercy .... You have been mindful of us in a wonderful manner, and have most graciously visited us in our helpless, lost, and ruined state. You have given your only begotten and well-beloved Son to be a ransom for our sins, and to suffer death upon the cross, the just for the unjust, that he might bring us to God (1 Pet. 3:18) .... Give us [now] a more lively sense of your mercies, and hearts more grateful to you for them. [49]

~Samuel Knight (1759–1827)

O what shall we render to the Lord for all his benefits! Dear Lord, let not our hearts be shut and [reticent] towards you, whose hand is every day so open unto us. But [fill] and enlarge these hearts of ours with more love and greater thankfulness to you. [50]

~Benjamin Jenks (1646-1724)

O Lord, from the bottom of my heart, I thank you for all your blessings, which you have bestowed upon my soul and body; for electing me in your love, redeeming me by your Son, sanctifying me by your Spirit, and preserving me from my youth up, until this present day and hour, by your most gracious providence. [51]

~Lewis Bayly (c.1575-1631)

What shall I render unto you, O blessed Savior, for all these blessings which you have so graciously bestowed upon my soul? How can I sufficiently thank you when I can scarcely express them? ... O blessed Redeemer, what an inestimable treasure of riches and overflowing fountain of grace have [I gained] in you! [52]

~Lewis Bayly (c.1575-1631)

Let my whole life be an expression of thankfulness unto you for your grace and mercy. [53]

~Lewis Bayly (c.1575-1631)

What shall I render to the LORD for all his benefits to me?... I will offer to you the sacrifice of thanksgiving and call on the name of the LORD. (Psa. 116:12, 17)

† † †

Pray Until You Pray

Even youths shall faint and be weary, and young men shall fall exhausted; but they who wait for the LORD shall renew their strength; they shall mount up with wings like eagles; they shall run and not be weary; they shall walk and not faint. (Isa. 40:30-31)

Pray for prayer—pray till you can pray; pray to be helped to pray, and give not up praying because you cannot pray, for it is when you think you *cannot pray* that you are *most praying*; and sometimes when you have no sort of comfort in your supplications, it is then that your heart, all broken and cast down, is really wrestling and truly prevailing with the Most High. [54]

~C.H. Spurgeon (1834-1892)

Many of the most blessed seasons of prayer I have ever known have begun with the feeling of utter deadness and prayerlessness; but in my helplessness and coldness I have cast myself upon God and looked to him to send his Holy Spirit to teach me to pray, and he has done it. [55]

~R.A. Torrey (1856-1928)

God may, and does sometimes conceal his enlivening presence, till the soul be engaged in the work .... Have you never launched out to [prayer] as the apostles to sea, with the wind on your teeth, as if the Spirit of God, instead of helping you on, meant to drive you back, and yet found Christ walking to you before the [prayer] was done? [56]

~William Gurnall (1616-1679)

The greater deadness and barrenness of your heart ... and the less hope you have to get out of [indifference], the more joyful will be the quickening presence of God to you. The assistance that thus surprises you beyond your expectation will be a true Isaac—a child of joy and laughter. [57]

~William Gurnall (1616-1679)

Our realization of the presence of God may, however, be accompanied with little or no emotion. Our spirits may lie as if dead under the hand of God. Vision and rapture may alike be withdrawn. But we ought not therefore to grow languid in prayer .... It may be that the prayer which goes up through darkness to God will bring to us a blessing such as we have not received in our most favored hours. [58]

~David McIntyre (1859-1938)

Do you not sometimes rise from your knees in your little room and say, "I do not think I have prayed. I could not feel at home in prayer?" Nine times out of every ten, those prayers are most prevalent with God which we think are the least acceptable. [59]

~C.H. Spurgeon (1834-1892)

You may mistake, and think your prayers weak, when they are strong. The strength of prayer consists not in anything outward, not in expressions either by word or tears, not in outward gestures or enlargements. It is a hidden, an inward strength. [60]

~David Clarkson (1622-1686)

It is a common temptation of Satan to make us give up the reading of the word and prayer when our enjoyment is gone; as if it were of no use .... The truth is, in order to enjoy the word, we ought to continue to read it, and the way to obtain a spirit of prayer is to continue praying. [61]

~George Müller (1805-1898)

I had fainted, unless I had believed to see the goodness of the LORD in the land of the living. Wait on the LORD: be of good courage, and he shall strengthen thine heart: wait, I say, on the LORD. (Psa. 27:13-14 KJV)

Help us, O Lord .... O give us renewed strength. May we rise as on eagles' wings to you, our God. May we run with patience; may we walk with steadfast perseverance in your ways. We continually ... feel the temptation to weariness and faintness. Bring your promises home to our hearts, that we may be preserved from being weary in well doing, knowing that we shall reap in due season if we faint not. [62]

~Edward Bickersteth (1786-1850)

Persist Through Every Distraction

I discipline my body and keep it under control. (1 Cor. 9:26-27)

What various hindrances we meet in coming to the mercy seat! Yet [he] that knows the worth of prayer but wishes to be often there! [63]

~William Cowper (1731-1800)

With me, every time of prayer, or almost every time, begins with a conflict. [64]

~Andrew Bonar (1810-1892)

When I would speak and pray to God by myself, a hundred thousand hindrances at once intervene before I get at it. Then the devil can throw all sorts of reasons for delay into my path; he can block and hinder me on all sides; as a result, I go my way and never think of [prayer] again. ... Try it. Resolve to pray earnestly, and no doubt you will see how large an assortment of your own thoughts will rush in on you and distract you, so that you cannot begin aright. [65]

~Martin Luther (1483-1546)

None knows how many bye-ways the heart has and back-lanes, to slip away from the presence of God. [66]

~John Bunyan (1628-1688)

How often, alas! do our souls begin to speak with God in prayer, and on a sudden [whim], fall chatting with the world! ... [One moment] we pursue hard after God with full cry of our affections, but instantly we are at a loss and hunt cold again. [67]

~William Gurnall (1616-1679)

The tempter hinders holy duty much by wandering thoughts, [depressing] perplexities, and a hurry of temptations which torment and distract some Christians so that they cry out, "I cannot pray, I cannot meditate," and are weary of duty, and even of their lives. This shows the malice of the tempter and your weakness; but if you [want to be] delivered from it, it does not hinder your acceptance with God. [68]

~Richard Baxter (1615-1691)

Prayer meets with obstacles, which must be prayed away. That is what men mean when they talk about *praying through*. [69]

~Albert Richardson (1868-19__)

To strive in prayer means in the final analysis to take up the battle against all the inner and outward hindrances which would dissociate us from the Spirit of prayer.[70]

~*O. Hallesby (1879-1961)*

Our [impulsive] spirits resist being pent up in the narrow room of [secret prayer]; we love to take our liberty in ranging abroad to a thousand other things. But Christian, as you love your peace, your soul, and your God, [guard] your spirit in secret prayer. Do not trifle away the time upon your knees.[71]

~*Oliver Heywood (1630-1702)*

"Watch and pray, that ye enter not into temptation." ... There is danger lest our minds and hearts should wander from God, when they should be fixed on him ... (Matt. 26:41). [Be] vigilant to prevent wanderings and distractions, those loose [impulses] of our vain minds and hearts into which they are apt to run when they should be most fixed.[72]

~*David Clarkson (1622-1686)*

[Do] not suffer diversions, but answer all foreign thoughts, as Nehemiah ... [to] them that would have called him off from building.[73]

~*William Gurnall (1616-1679)*

I am doing a great work and I cannot come down. Why should the work stop while I leave it and come down to you? (Neh. 6:3)

When blasphemous or disturbing thoughts look in or fruitless musings, presently meet them, and use that authority of reason which is left you, to cast them and command them out.[74]

~*Richard Baxter (1615-1691)*

O Lord, we do not find it easy to get rid of distracting thoughts, but we ask you to help us draw the sword against them and drive them away.[75]

~C.H. Spurgeon (1834-1892)

Teach me your way, O LORD, that I may walk in your truth; unite my heart to fear your name. (Psa. 86:11)

"Unite my heart to fear your name." It is the natural disease of man's heart to be loosed from God, and to be distracted in variety of worldly objects, which obtrude themselves upon our senses [and] offer themselves to us daily.[76]

~Thomas Manton (1620-1677)

Go to God, then, [asking] him to keep your heart together; he that has set bounds to the sea and can bind up the waves in a heap, ... certainly he can fasten and establish your heart, and keep it from running out.[77]

~Thomas Manton (1620-1677)

Let no beginner in prayer abandon the privilege because of mind-wandering. It can be conquered .... Even though, in the early stages, the precious minutes tick away and all the time seems spent in bringing the mind back from its wanderings and fixing it again on prayer, they are not moments lost. Such discipline will exercise the muscles of the will, and the day will dawn when the sweetest meditation and the most earnest prayer will be possible even amid distraction.[78]

~William E. Sangster (1900-1960)

The difficulty of praying without distraction, and the fact that distractions do mingle with our holiest services, should [instill in us] many practical lessons; such as humility, brokenness of spirit, ... entire dependence on Christ for righteousness and strength, breathings after the influence of the Spirit, and a longing to be in heaven, where all our services will be pure and holy. That prayer is not lost which produces any of these effects. No, if a distracted prayer does but deeply humble us, it may be one of our most profitable prayers.[79]

~*Edward Bickersteth (1786-1850)*

Ah dearest Lord, I cannot pray, my fancy is not free;

Unmannerly distractions come, and force my thoughts from thee.

The world that looks so dull all day glows bright on me at prayer,

And plans that ask no thought but then wake up and meet me there ....

I cannot pray; yet, Lord, thou knowest the pain it is to me

To have my vainly struggling thoughts thus torn away from thee ....

Yet thou art oft most present, Lord, in weak distracted prayer:

A sinner out of heart with self, most often finds thee there.

For prayer that humbles sets the soul from all illusions free,

And teaches it how utterly, dear Lord, it hangs on thee.[80]

~*Fredrick W. Faber (1814-1863)*

O Lord, we bring before you our great difficulty and trouble in the midst of our religious privileges .... Our minds are carnal, worldly, and earthly. Our souls cleave to the dust. Innumerable vain imaginations and worldly thoughts distract and fill our minds; we lose the sense of your nearness, and with the words of prayer on our lips, have innumerable vanities possessing our inner man. Send your mighty Spirit into our hearts to effectually aid us against Satan and our inward foes. May we this day know the power, and reality, and glory of true prayer.[81]

~*Edward Bickersteth (1786-1850)*

Four

Steps after Prayer

✝ ✝ ✝

Believe God Accepts Your Prayer

The prayer of the upright is his delight. ✝ The LORD has heard my plea; the LORD accepts my prayer. (Prov. 15:8 KJV; Psa. 6:9)

You have in prayer labored to [prevail with] God to hear and help you; now take as much pains to overcome your heart into a quiet waiting on God and entire confidence in him. [1]

~*William Gurnall (1616-1679)*

O what astonishing damps are upon my trembling spirit, when I rise off my knees and think, "Will God hear such a distracted prayer of a poor hard-hearted wretch?" Surely conscience says, "no." But what does faith say? A poor trembling faith puts [my prayer] into the hands of my Advocate, and then says, "He can make something of it." My eyes are fastened upon him at God's right hand, and thereby faith is elevated, and despair gradually vanishes. [2]

~*Oliver Heywood (1630-1702)*

In the best prayer that was ever offered by the holiest man that ever lived, there was enough sin in it to render it a polluted thing if the Lord had looked upon it by itself .... Our consolation lies in this—that our beloved Intercessor who stands before God for us, even Christ Jesus—possesses such an abundance of precious merit, that he puts fragrance into our supplications, and imparts a delicious aroma to our prayers![3]

~C.H. Spurgeon (1834-1892)

God allows the most vile and unworthy, the greatest sinners ... to come through Christ. And he not only allows, but encourages, and frequently invites them, ... delighting in being sought [after] by prayer (Prov. 15:8) .... "O my dove, let me hear thy voice; for sweet is thy voice" (Song 2:14).[4]

~Jonathan Edwards (1703-1758)

The fact is that sincere prayer may often be very feeble to us, but it is always acceptable to God .... [Our prayers] are foul with unbelief, decayed with [foolishness], and worm-eaten with wandering thoughts; but nevertheless, God accepts them at heaven's own bank, and gives us rich and ready blessings, in return for our supplications.[5]

~C.H. Spurgeon (1834-1892)

We are sometimes tempted to think that we get no good by our prayers, and that we may as well give them up altogether. Let us resist the temptation. It comes from the devil. Let us believe, and pray on. Against our besetting sins, against the spirit of the world, against the wiles of the devil, let us pray on, and not faint. For strength to do duty, for grace to bear our trials, for comfort in every trouble, let us continue in prayer. Let us be sure that no time is so well spent in every day, as that which we spend upon our knees. Jesus hears us, and in his own good time will give an answer.[6]

~J.C. Ryle (1816-1900)

Jesus, my strength, my hope, on thee I cast my care,
With humble confidence look up, and know thou hearest my
prayer.[7]

~Charles Wesley (1707-1788)

O you who hear prayer—unto you we now come. Grant that
by the eye of faith we may behold you bending down your ear
of love to receive our feeble breathings. May our cries ascend
perfumed with the incense of Jesus' atoning blood, and so
be welcomed with acceptance. We shall prevail, for you have
promised. Smiles await us, for your Spirit intercedes within us.
We shall be heard, for your dear Son pleads for us.[8]

~Henry Law (1797-1884)

† † †

Keep Walking in the Attitude of Prayer

*Pray without ceasing. † Praying at all times in the Spirit.
(1 Th. 5:17; Eph. 6:18)*

He that prays constantly has set times every day for prayer ....
The Christian has his set meals for his soul every day as well as
for his body. With the marigold, he opens himself in the morning for the sweet dews of heaven's grace and blessing, and he
does at night ... like a lover, find some opportunity to converse
with his beloved.[9]

~George Swinnock (1627-1673)

[Let us] supplement those times [of private prayer] by a thousand thought-prayers as we go about the job of living. Let us
practice the fine art of making every work a priestly ministra-

tion. Let us believe that God is in all our simple deeds and learn to find him there. [10]

~A. W. Tozer (1897-1963)

Fellowship with God as an *activity* will issue into fellowship with God as an *attitude*. When this is so, anywhere, and at any moment, and in any method [our] spirit will speak its need in the listening ear of God. Our fathers used to speak of and practice ejaculatory prayer. It would be a great gain to all of us if we could learn again the method and practice it. [11]

~G. Campbell Morgan (1863-1945)

Into all our daily duties, dear friends, however absorbing, however secular, however small, however irritating they may be, however monotonous, into all our daily duties it is possible to bring [our God]. [12]

~Alexander Maclaren (1826-1910)

I have set the LORD always before me. (Psa. 16:8)

If the Apostle wills "that men pray always," (1 Tim. 2:8) it must be possible while going about business, study, daily work, [and] work at home amongst the children ... not only to pray while we are working, but to *make work prayer*, which is even better .... If in all that I do, I try to realize my dependence on God for power; to look to him for direction, and to trust him for [strength], then whether I eat, or drink, or pray, or study, or buy and sell, or marry or am given in marriage, all will be worship of God. [13]

~Alexander Maclaren (1826-1910)

Whatever you may be saying or doing, however head, heart, hands may be occupied, *be praying always* in the spirit of your sayings and doings [and] in your pervading temper and disposition. [14]

~James Hastings (1852-1922)

The believer's spirit is like fire upon the hearth; though it does not blaze, yet it is ready upon any opportunity to be blown up into a flame.... In all things let your requests be made known to God. When you rise up or lie down, when you go out or come in, prayer must still be with you.[15]

~George Swinnock (1627-1673)

[A Christian] may pray continually. No place, no company can deprive him of this privilege. If he be on the top of a house with Peter, he may pray; if he be in the bottom of the ocean with Jonah, he may pray; if he be walking in the field with Isaac, he may pray when no eye sees him; if he be waiting at table with Nehemiah, he may pray when no ear hears him; if he be in the mountains with our Savior, he may pray; if he be in the prison with Paul, he may pray; wherever he is, prayer will help him to find God out. Every saint is God's temple; and he that carries his temple about him ... may go to prayer when he pleases. Indeed, to a Christian, every house is a house of prayer; every closet a chamber of presence; and every place he comes to an altar, whereon he may offer the sacrifice of prayer.[16]

~George Swinnock (1627-1673)

God has this week been impressing much upon me the way of redeeming time for prayer by learning to pray while walking or going from place to place.[17]

~Andrew Bonar (1810-1892)

I have been endeavoring to keep up prayer at this season every hour of the day, stopping my occupation, whatever it is, to pray a little, seeking thus to keep my soul within the shadow of the throne of grace and him that sits thereon.[18]

~Andrew Bonar (1810-1892)

When [I] have been for some time interrupted in [my] great work, and thoughts of God have been diverted, how pleasing it is to the mind to feel the motions of his Spirit quickening [me] and exciting [me] to return.[19]

~Susanna Wesley (1669-1742),

By practice, remembering God as much as we can, and asking him to forgive us when we had passed long hours in forgetfulness of him, this habit would become easy and natural to us—a kind of second nature. ... How much they miss, who only speak to God from their knees, or on set occasions! There must be such times for us all; but we may link them together by a perpetual ripple of holy and loving converse with him who counts the hairs of our heads in his minute microscopic interest in our concerns.[20]

~F.B. Meyer (1847-1929),

O blessed person! I hope there are many such persons among you, whose life is a continued prayer, as David who gave himself to prayer (Psa. 109:4) .... He is all over prayer: prays at rising, prays at lying down, prays as he walks; he is always ready for prayer.[21]

~Samuel Lee (1625-1691)

There is not in the world a kind of life more sweet and delightful than that of a continual conversation with God.[22]

~Brother Lawrence (1614-1691)

Oh, the sweet delights of constancy in prayer! ... Be always praying. Is that possible? Some have realized it, till the whole of the engagements of the day have been ablaze with prayer .... Blessed are we when prayer surrounds us like an atmosphere.[23]

~C.H. Spurgeon (1834-1892)

Sudden dartings of the soul heavenward, ... [will] be answered with frequent beams of God's countenance returned to the soul .... It pleases God thus to keep intercourse with those souls that love him, ... interchanging as it were sudden glances of love. (Song 4:9)[24]

~Robert Leighton (1611-1684)

[O Lord], possess us with the Spirit of grace, which is always a Spirit of supplication. May we live in a prayerful frame of mind, that will always allow of our immediate and pleasing intercourse with you; in the ordinary concerns of life may our thoughts and desires often ascend to the skies. [25]

~William Jay (1769-1853)

† † †

Persevere in the Habit of Prayer

Do not be slothful in zeal, be fervent in spirit, serve the Lord. Rejoice in hope, be patient in tribulation, be constant in prayer.
(Rom. 12:11-12)

The command to continue in prayer is not an easy thing. It can mean conflict, wrestling, agony. Forces are moving in the unseen [realm] about us, and prayer influences those movements …. Lord, help us to continue, to persevere in prayer. Hold our hands steady until the going down of the sun. (Ex. 17:12) [26]

~Amy Carmichael (1867-1951)

Prayer is the putting forth of vital energy. It is the highest effort of which the human spirit is capable. Efficiency and power in prayer cannot be obtained without patient continuance and much practice. [27]

~Andrew Murray (1828-1917)

It is far more easy to begin a habit of prayer than to keep it up …. Thousands take up a habit of praying for a little season, after some special mercy or special affliction, and then little by little become cold about it, and at last lay it aside. The secret thought comes stealing over men's minds that it is no use to pray. They see no visible benefit from it. They persuade themselves that they get on just as well without prayer. Laziness and unbelief prevail over their hearts, and at last they altogether "restrain prayer before God" (Job 15:4). Let us resist this feeling, whenever we feel it rising within us. Let us resolve by God's grace, that however poor and feeble our prayers may seem to be, we will pray on. It is not for nothing that the Bible tells us so frequently, to "watch unto prayer," to "pray without ceasing," to "continue in prayer," to "pray always and not to faint," to be "instant in prayer."[28]

~J.C. Ryle (1816-1900)

Once having begun the habit [of prayer] never give it up ....
Your body will sometimes say, "You are unwell, or sleepy, or weary; you need not pray." Your mind will sometimes say, "You have important business to attend to today; cut short your prayers." Look on all such suggestions as coming direct from Satan. They are all as good as saying, "Neglect your soul."[29]

~J.C. Ryle (1816-1900)

[Postponing] communion with God, for whatever cause, only makes [it] more difficult [to resume and recover] the prayer habit and prayer spirit; whereas the persistent outpouring of supplication, together with continued activity in the service of God, soon brings back the lost joy. Whenever, therefore, one yields to spiritual depression so as to abandon, or even to suspend, closet communion or Christian work, the devil triumphs.[30]

~A.T. Pierson (1837-1911)

Satan is ever laboring to draw us off from our prayers and filling our minds with reasons why we may give them up. These things are true with respect to all prayers, but they are especially true with respect to intercessory prayer. It is always far more meager than it ought to be. It is often attempted for a little season, and then left off. We see no immediate answer to our prayers. We see the people for whose souls we pray, going on still in sin. We draw the conclusion that it is useless to pray for them and allow our intercession to come to an end. [31]

~J.C. Ryle (1816-1900)

[But] let us name all whom we love before God continually .... Let us continue praying for them year after year, in spite of their continued unbelief. God's time of mercy may be a distant one. Our eyes may not see an answer to our intercessions. The answer may not come for ten, fifteen, or twenty years. It may not come till we have exchanged prayer for praise and are far away from this world. But while we live, let us pray for others. [32]

~J.C. Ryle (1816-1900)

Day after day, and year after year, by the help of God, we labor in prayer for the spiritual benefit of the orphans under our care. These our supplications, which have been for twenty-four years brought before the Lord concerning them, have been abundantly answered ... in the conversion of hundreds from among them .... [What] a most precious answer to prayer. [33]

~George Müller (1805-1898)

Whoever has made it a practice to spend certain hours or half-hours in the day alone with God, knows the extraordinary effect produced by the gradual accumulation of experiences, and the settled habit of the soul. ... The habit in long years secures a remarkable result. [34]

~R.F. Horton (1855-1934)

Pray on, pray on, believing ones, God's promised word is sure,
That they shall overcome by faith who to the end endure;
Pray on, pray on, O weary not; the cross with patience bear,
And though its burden weigh us down, the Lord will answer prayer. [35]

~Fanny Crosby (1820-1915)

We should unite in our practice these two things which our Savior unites in his precept: *praying* and *not fainting* (Luke 18:1)

.... It is very apparent from the word of God, that he is [accustomed] often to try the faith and patience of his people, when crying to him for some great and important mercy, by withholding the mercy sought, for a season; and not only so, but at first to cause an increase of dark appearances. And yet he, without fail, at last succeeds those who continue [constant] in prayer with all perseverance, and "will not let him go except he blesses." [36]

~Jonathan Edwards (1703-1758)

Depend upon him that gives power to the faint and increases strength in them that have no might. He faints not, neither is he weary, and he alone can keep you from being weary in well doing. As he only can help you when you cry, so he alone can help you to hold on in crying. Cheer up yourselves with this consideration, that if you persevere in prayer but a little while longer, in heaven all your prayers will be fully answered, ... and prayer will end in everlasting praises. [37]

~Nathaniel Vincent (c.1639-1697)

[Remember] Christ himself [as] an example beyond all example .... He has been already above a thousand years there [in heaven] at prayer for his church, and against his enemies, and has not yet received the full of his desires; but still is expecting till the one be saved, and the other be made his footstool. [38]

~William Gurnall (1616-1679)

[Lord God], apart from your dear Son, we are nothing, and can do nothing. Left to ourselves, our desires languish, our hearts relapse to deadness, our hands hang down, our efforts wither as a blighted blossom. But leave us not—we meekly pray .... Give us patience, remembering your marvelous forbearance. Your love to us has never wearied. Strengthen us that we may never weary in well-doing, knowing that in due season we shall reap—if we faint not. [39]

~Henry Law (1797-1884)

Part II

Approaching the Triune God in Prayer

For through [Christ] we both have access in one Spirit to the Father.
(Eph. 2:18)

No tongue can express, no mind can reach, the heavenly [tranquility] and soul-satisfying delight which are intimated in these words [of Ephesians 2:18]. How full of sweetness and satisfaction it is to come to God as a Father, through Christ, by the help and assistance of the Holy Spirit![1]

~*John Owen (1616-1683)*

Only think of it! The triune God takes part in every prayer: the Father who hears, the Son in whose name we pray, and the Spirit who prays for us and in us.[2]

~*Andrew Murray (1828-1917)*

God is [our] Father, willing to hear prayers; Christ is [our] Advocate, willing to present [our] requests in court; and the Spirit a notary to indite and draw up [our] requests for [us].[3]

~*Thomas Manton (1620-1677)*

The three divine persons have all cooperated in opening the gates of prayer …. The whole Trinity [works] in our behalf.[4]

~*A.B. Simpson (1843-1919)*

We now have to ask ourselves, "What is the revelation of the Father; what [is] the mediation of the Son; what [is] the inspiration of the Spirit?" We need to examine these things in order to

find out how far we are responsive to them ... [and] how far we
are really prepared for prayer.[5]

~G. Campbell Morgan (1863-1945)

May our hearts be fitted for the indwelling of our majestic God
.... Holy, blessed, and glorious Trinity, three persons and one
God—inhabit us as temples consecrated to your glory.[6]

~Henry Law (1797-1884)

Five

Praying to the Father

† † †

We Approach God as Father

But when you pray, go into your room and shut the door and pray to your Father who is in secret.... Pray then like this: "Our Father in heaven." (Matt. 6:6-9)

[Prayer] is not the cry of nature to an unknown God, but the intelligent converse of a child with his heavenly Father. [1]

~*A.B. Simpson (1843-1919)*

It is best for each one, when he goes into his closet and begins to pray, to make an effort to understand what he is saying, and properly to weigh two words, "Our Father." ... Do you truly regard God as your Father, and yourself as his dear child? [2]

~*Martin Luther (1483-1546)*

The essence of true prayer is found in the two words, "Our Father," ... [yet] it is just this realization of our relationship to God that we so sadly lack. [3]

~*Martyn Lloyd-Jones (1899-1981)*

[If] you complain of smallness, lifelessness, and reluctance in devotion, ... may not the cause be found in the imperfect realization of your adoption, in the faint conception you have of the parental relation of God to you, in the little filial affection and confidence which marks your approach to the throne of grace? Remember that true prayer is nothing less than the warm, confidential communion of a believing child with God. [4]

~Octavius Winslow (1808-1878)

O that we realized this! If only we realized that this almighty God is our Father through our Lord Jesus Christ. If only we realized that we are indeed his children and whenever we pray it is like a child going to its father! He knows all about us; he knows our every need before we tell him. As a father cares for the child and looks at the child, is concerned about the child and anticipates the needs of the child, so is God with respect to all those who are in Christ Jesus. He desires to bless us very much more than we desire to be blessed. [5]

~Martyn Lloyd-Jones (1899-1981)

[Father], what an unspeakable mercy it is that creatures so sinful and so perverse and ungrateful as we have been, can yet … come into your holy presence, and know that you are reconciled to us by the cross of Jesus, and will receive us as your sons and your daughters. [6]

~Edward Bickersteth (1786-1850)

† † †

Our Father is Good and Gracious toward His Children

Therefore the LORD waits to be gracious to you, and therefore he exalts himself to show mercy to you. (Isa. 30:18)

The wonderful [effectiveness] of prayer depends not upon the nature of our petitions or the temper of our soul, but the goodness of God to whom we [pray] …. He loves to have an opportunity to manifest his affection above the [generosity] and tenderness of worldly fathers.[7]

~Stephen Charnock (1628-1680)

Our heavenly Father's love [is] the archetype of all parental affection. [It] is tainted by no evil and darkened by no ignorance. He loves perfectly and wisely.[8]

~Alexander Maclaren (1826-1910)

Which one of you, if his son asks him for bread, will give him a stone? Or if he asks for a fish, will give him a serpent? If you then, who are evil, know how to give good gifts to your children, how much more will your Father who is in heaven give good things to those who ask him!
† *How much more will the heavenly Father give the Holy Spirit to those who ask him! (Matt. 7:9-11; Luke 11:13)*

That passage of Scripture [in Luke 11:13] occurred to my mind, and gave me great assistance [in prayer] …. I was helped to plead [this text] and insist upon [it, for I] saw the divine faithfulness engaged for dealing with me better than any earthly parent can do with his child.[9]

~David Brainerd (1718-1747)

[O Lord], still be a gracious Father to me and a merciful Provider for me, and grant me now the comfortable sense of your gracious acceptance of me and of your [plans] of mercy towards me. Be pleased to take me under your fatherly care and conduct. Preserve me from the evils into which I am prone to fall. [Enliven] me to the good which I am averse to perform .... Hold me up, and I shall be safe. (Psa. 119:117) [10]

~Benjamin Jenks (1646-1724)

[Some saints] are afraid to have good thoughts of God. They think it a boldness to eye God as good, gracious, tender, kind, loving .... Is not this soul-deceit from Satan? Was it not his design from the beginning to inject such [wrong] thoughts of God? (cf. Gen. 3:5) [11]

~John Owen (1616-1683)

We know that God is holy. We know he is just. We believe that he can be angry with them that go on still in sin. But we also believe that to those who draw near to him in Christ Jesus, he is most merciful, most loving, and most tender, most compassionate. [12]

~J.C. Ryle (1816-1900)

Let it be most deeply engraved on your heart, that God is infinitely good and amiable; your grand Benefactor and Father in Christ. [13]

~Richard Baxter (1615-1691)

[Let us] draw near to God in prayer, ... [for] God is ready and willing to help us, and we should come to him in that confidence. We should pour out our hearts into his bosom, in full confidence of his pity. Whom can a child expect help of, if not of a father? But no father has the bowels of compassion that God has toward his own. [14]

~Thomas Boston (1676-1732)

Father of mercies, ... O the inconceivable depths of goodness that are in your gracious nature! ... How good you have been to my soul. O that these wonders of love may ... bring me nearer to [you] and make me more to abound in your love! [15]

~Benjamin Jenks (1646-1724)

[Father], it seems to us impossible not to love you, for you are so supremely lovable, so full of goodness, so perfect .... Be pleased today to fill us with delight because of your love. [16]

~*C.H. Spurgeon (1834-1892)*

✝ ✝ ✝

Our Father Loves and Pities His Children

See what kind of love the Father has given to us, that we should be called children of God; and so we are. (1 John 3:1)

What manner of love is this, that we should now be called the children of God .... That [we] poor creatures, whenever [we] have but a heart to step aside, and give God a visit in any corner of [our] house, should find the arms of so great a majesty open to embrace [us]! — this is so stupendous that we may better admire than express it .... O thank our good friend and brother, the Lord Jesus Christ, for this! It is he that brings us into the presence of God, and sets us before his face. [17]

~*William Gurnall (1616-1679)*

In this is love, not that we have loved God but that he loved us and sent his Son to be the propitiation for our sins. (1 John 4:10)

[The Father] so loved that he gave his only-begotten Son (John 3:16) .... He has loved you unto the death of his Son. Upon him he laid your sins; of him he exacted your penalty; into his cup he pressed all the bitterness of your death and all the ingredients of your condemnation .... Doubt not the love of your Father in heaven, who surrendered his only and well-beloved Son unto the death for you! [18]

~*Octavius Winslow (1808-1878)*

As a father shows compassion to his children, so the LORD
shows compassion to those who fear him. For he knows
our frame; he remembers that we are dust. (Psa. 103:13-14)

We are his own children. Oh! I have found it such a blessed
thing, in my own experience, to plead before God that I am his
child …. When we are lowest, we can still say, "Our Father,"
and when it is very dark, and we are very weak, our childlike
appeal can go up, "Father, help me! Father rescue me!" [19]

~C.H. Spurgeon (1834-1892)

If [we] but put forth in prayer that little strength [we] have, God
would quickly renew [our] spiritual strength; he would certainly carry [us] on from strength to strength …. As a loving and
caring father will take his little child in his arms, and carry him
on in his way homeward, when his strength begins to fail him,
and he can walk no further … so does God. (Hos. 11:3) [20]

~Thomas Brooks (1608-1680)

You have seen how the LORD your God carried you, as a
man carries his son, all the way that you went until you
came to this place. (Deut. 1:31)

Let [the] wonderful revelation of a Father's tenderness free all
young Christians from every thought of secret prayer as a duty
or a burden, and lead them to regard it as the highest privilege
of their life, a joy and a blessing. [21]

~Andrew Murray (1828-1917)

Father-like he tends and spares us; well our feeble frame he knows.
In his hands he gently bears us, rescues us from all our foes.
Alleluia! Alleluia! Widely yet his mercy flows! [22]

~Henry Lyte (1793-1847)

[O Father], look in pity upon our many sins, weaknesses and
infirmities. May we fully believe and prove the power of your
word, that as a father pities his children, so the Lord pities them

that fear him. O pity our deadness and dullness in your service; pity our backwardness and aversion to divine and heavenly things; pity all our weakness and helplessness; ... and heal, O heal all our spiritual diseases.[23]

~Edward Bickersteth (1786-1850)

† † †
Our Father Disciplines His Children

My son, do not regard lightly the discipline of the Lord, nor be weary when reproved by him. † *For the* LORD *reproves him whom he loves, as a father the son in whom he delights. (Heb. 12:5; Prov. 3:12)*

[A wise and loving father will not] neglect the training of his child, and some day that child will bless his memory for a father's firm and faithful love. So, God our Father sends us to the school of discipline, of suffering, of life's severe experience.[24]

~A.B. Simpson (1843-1919)

And I will put this third into the fire, and refine them as one refines silver, and test them as gold is tested. They will call upon my name, and I will answer them. (Zech. 13:9)

Hard places teach us to pray .... They drove Jacob to his knees at the fords of Jabbok (cf. Gen. 32). They taught David to find the secret place of the Most High (cf. Psa. 91). They made the life of Paul one ceaseless dependence upon the presence of his Lord (cf. 2 Cor. 12), and they have inspired [and] sustained the divine communion which most of us have learned to prove as the supreme resource and solution of our lives.[25]

~A.B. Simpson (1843-1919)

The rod is sent ... [and] it awakens the slumbering affections of the soul. Then the chastened child cries out to God. The spirit of prayer, so long stagnant, is stirred up. The heart so cold and torpid is set upon seeking the Lord …. May this be the [holy] and happy issue of your present trial! [26]

~*Octavius Winslow (1808-1878)*

[When] the rod of your heavenly Father is upon you … will you flee from [your] Father … [or will you] hasten and throw yourself into his arms, and fall upon his bosom, confessing your sins, and imploring his forgiveness? … Blessed is the man, O Lord, whom you chasten, and draw closer within … [your] sheltering bosom! [27]

~*Octavius Winslow (1808-1878)*

Loving you, the Father yearns to clasp you to his bosom, assuring you that you are his loved, pardoned, accepted child. [28]

~*Octavius Winslow (1808-1878)*

When we cannot understand his hand let us always lie close to his heart. [29]

~*A.B. Simpson (1843-1919)*

[Let us] draw these conclusions: [my Father] designs my good by all the hardships I am under (Rom. 8:28); he pities me under them (Psa. 103:13); [and] he knows the best time for removing them, and will do it, when that comes. (Lam. 3:31-32) [30]

~*Thomas Boston (1676-1732)*

Though he cause grief, he will have compassion. (Lam. 3:32)

[O Father], how patiently and skillfully have you taught me! I could not have done without your teaching and your discipline …. I have stumbled, and you have upheld me. I have fallen, and you have raised me up. I have wandered, and you have restored. I have wounded myself, and you have healed me. Oh, what a God have you been to me! What a Father! [31]

~*Octavius Winslow (1808-1878)*

† † †

Our Father is Revealed by Jesus and the Spirit

*I have manifested your name .... I made known to them your name,
and I will continue to make it known, that the love with which you
have loved me may be in them, and I in them.* (John 17:6, 26)

[Jesus] came to earth as the Revealer of the Father and the
Father's name. He knew that name well; and when he said,
"Abba, Father," and "righteous Father," and "holy Father," and
"our Father," he spoke as one who knew it [and] as one who was
seeking to make others know it. [32]

~Horatius Bonar (1808-1889)

How tender and touching were his words—"I ascend unto my
Father, and your Father; and to my God, and your God." (John
20:17) ... Oh, claim the dignity and privilege of your birthright!
Approach God as your father. "Abba, Father!" How tender the
relation! How intense the affection! What power it imparts to
prayer! [33]

~Octavius Winslow (1808-1878)

We have a ... claim to sonship by virtue of our union with Christ,
the only begotten Son of God. Wedded to him, we come into
his peculiar sonship .... As a bride inherits her husband's home
and is accepted as a child, so we go in with him to the innermost
chambers of the palace of the King [and] hear him say, "My
Father, and your Father; my God, and your God" (John 20:17). [34]

~A.B. Simpson (1843-1919)

Taking us by the hand, [Jesus] gently leads us to God and bids
us call him "Father." [35]

~Octavius Winslow (1808-1878)

And because you are sons, God has sent the Spirit of his
Son into our hearts, crying, "Abba! Father!" (Gal. 4:6)

The Holy Spirit is called *the Spirit of his Son* .... We do well to
ponder [this name] long until we realize the glad fullness of its
significance.[36]

~*R.A. Torrey (1856-1928)*

The natural attitude of our hearts towards God is not that of
sons .... But when the Spirit of his Son bears witness together
with our spirit to our sonship, then we are filled and thrilled
with the sense that we are sons![37]

~*R.A. Torrey (1856-1928)*

God our Father longs that we [should] know and realize that
we are his sons. He longs to hear us call him, "Father" from
hearts that realize what they say, and that trust him without
fear or anxiety .... When we look up into [our Father's] face
and from a heart which the Holy Spirit has filled with a sense of
sonship call him, "Abba ... Father," no language can describe
the joy of God.[38]

~*R.A. Torrey (1856-1928)*

My son, ... my inmost being will exult when your lips
speak what is right. (Prov. 23:16)

The Spirit of adoption ... [assures you] that he is an omnipotent
Father, so *can* do all things; that he is a compassionate Father, so
will do all things; ... [and] that he is a wise Father, so [he] *orders*
everything *for the best.*[39]

~*Anthony Burgess (1600-1663)*

O heavenly Father, ... send your Holy Spirit into my heart,
which may assure me that you are my Father, and that I am
your child, and that you love me with an unchangeable love.[40]

~*Lewis Bayly (c.1575-1631)*

† † †

Let Us Pray to Our Father

I bow my knees before the Father. † *Indeed our fellowship is with the Father and with his Son Jesus Christ. (Eph. 3:14; 1 John 1:3)*

We have access to the Father .... Are we enjoying this access?[41]
~*Martyn Lloyd-Jones (1899-1981)*

Come to the inner chamber because your Father with his love awaits you there. Although you are cold, dark, sinful; although it is doubtful whether you can pray at all; come, because the Father is there, and there looks upon you. Set yourself beneath the light of his eye. Believe in his tender fatherly love, and out of this faith prayer will be born. (Matt. 6:8; 7:11)[42]
~*Andrew Murray (1828-1917)*

Pray to your Father who is in secret; and your Father who sees in secret shall reward you openly. We should well imagine and realize that there should be no place on earth so attractive to the child of God as the inner chamber, with the presence of God promised, where we can have unhindered communion with the Father .... [There] you can communicate with your God as long and as intimately as you desire; you can rely on his presence and fellowship.[43]
~*Andrew Murray (1828-1917)*

[When you pray], of more importance than all your requests ... is this one thing—the childlike, living assurance that your Father sees you, that you have now met him, and that with his eye on you and yours on him, you are now enjoying actual fellowship with him.[44]
~*Andrew Murray (1828-1917)*

The enjoyment of the fatherly love of God is the highest happiness in which the soul does rest content. [45]

~Thomas Manton (1620-1677)

[May we be] swallowed up in the admiration of such exceeding great benevolence and love of God, our heavenly Father. [46]

~John Bradford (1510-1555)

Exercise your thoughts upon this very thing, the eternal, free, and fruitful love of the Father, and see if your hearts be not [moved] to delight in him …. Sit down a little at the fountain, and you will quickly have a further discovery of the sweetness of the streams. [47]

~John Owen (1616-1683)

The Lord is mindful of us and visits us at every turn …. He does not forget us. Oh, let us not forget God. Let us manifest our love, by being often with him at the throne of grace, with our Father which is in heaven. A child is never [more pleased] but when in the mother's lap or under the father's wing. So should it be with us, with a humble affection coming into the presence of God and getting into the bosom of our heavenly Father. Never delight in anything so much as conversing with him, and serious addresses to him in prayer. [48]

~Thomas Manton (1620-1677)

Let us therefore draw near to him … for as often as we may draw near, we shall see him awaiting our movements. And if we fail to draw from his ever-springing goodness, the blame is all ours. [49]

~John Chrysostom (347-407)

[O God], what manner of love is this, that we who have been rebels against heaven, slaves of Satan, and children of wrath, should be made the children of the Most High, and heirs of everlasting glory! … You are our Father; O that we may with confidence and delight draw near unto you as dear children! [50]

~Benjamin Jenks (1646-1724)

Six

Praying through the Son

† † †

We Stand in Need of a Mediator

Who is able to stand before the LORD, this holy God? † Depart from me, for I am a sinful man, O Lord. (1 Sam. 6:20; Luke 5:8)

Vast is the distance [between] God and man, as we are his creatures, worms at his footstool, but he is "the blessed and only Potentate, King of kings, and Lord of lords, who only hath immortality, dwelling in that light which no man can approach unto" (1 Tim. 6:15-16). The highest seraphim cover their faces, as not able to behold the glory of his majesty. O how much less is such a clod of earth able to draw near to him?[1]

~*Oliver Heywood (1630-1702)*

But then consider what further distance sin has produced, [between] the holy God and such impure beings as we are; "God is of purer eyes than to behold evil, and cannot look on iniquity" (Hab. 1:13). And what are we but masses of sin? How can we then expect that God, this sin-hating God, should look towards us with any respect? Surely a glance of his eye would confound us.[2]

~*Oliver Heywood (1630-1702)*

Be sensible of your sin, and you will no more attempt to approach [the] absolute Deity than you would walk into a volcano's mouth. You will feel that you need a sacrifice, a propitiation, a Savior, a Mediator.[3]

~C.H. Spurgeon (1834-1892)

Till God in human flesh I see, my thoughts no comfort find; The holy, just, and sacred Three are terrors to my mind.

But if Immanuel's face appear, my hope, my joy begins; His name forbids my slavish fear, his grace removes my sins.[4]

~Isaac Watts (1674-1748)

There is no access for a sinful creature to God without a Mediator (Isa. 59:2; John 14:6). Sin has set us at a distance from God, and has bolted the door of our access to him. It is beyond our power or that of any creature to open it for us.[5]

~Thomas Boston (1676-1732)

But, look! The flaming sword guarding the way to the tree of life is seen quenched with blood. The unbridged gulf of separation has been spanned .... God was in Christ reconciling a lost world to himself. (2 Cor. 5:19)[6]

~John MacDuff (1818-1895)

[Now whoever] comes by Jesus Christ ... finds an open door of access to God and communion with him. The flaming sword he finds removed, and ... now a consuming fire he finds a warming sun to his soul.[7]

~Thomas Boston (1676-1732)

We owe it to [Christ's] intercession that we are here alive this day. [If he] did not interpose, we would be gone .... "Cut them down," says justice. "Let them alone," says Jesus. And thus it is, we are left alone.[8]

~Philip Henry (1631-1696)

Look upon me, O Father, through the merits and mediation of Jesus Christ, your beloved Son, in whom only you are well pleased! For of myself, I am not worthy to stand in your presence, or to speak with my unclean lips to so holy a God as you are.[9]

~Lewis Bayly (c.1575-1631)

† † †

Jesus Stands Between as Our Mediator

Jesus said to him, "I am the way, and the truth, and the life. No one comes to the Father except through me." † There is one mediator between God and men, the man Christ Jesus.
(John 14:6; 1 Tim. 2:5)

All that passes between a just God and poor sinners must pass through the hands of that blessed Arbiter, who has laid his hand upon them both (Job 9:33); every prayer passes from us to God, and every mercy from God to us, by that hand …. Therefore, [let us] make mention of his righteousness, even of his only.[10]

~Matthew Henry (1662-1714)

[Let us] hide ourselves behind the Lord Jesus, for we and our prayers can only be accepted in the Beloved, through the Person, the merit, the sacrifice, the ever-living intercession of the Lord Jesus Christ.[11]

~C.H. Spurgeon (1834-1892)

[Christ] alone is our mouth, by whom we speak to God. He is our eyes, by whom we see God, and also our right hand, by whom we offer anything unto the Father.[12]

~Ambrose of Milan (c. 340-397)

The Lord delights to be reminded of his Son's excellencies—it is a theme that he delights in! You may ring that bell as long as you ever will—the Father will never weary of it. Tell him what his Son has done; remind him of Gethsemane; bring up before the Father's mind the cross of Calvary .... Everything about Christ is sweet to God, and because believers' prayers are full of Christ, therefore they are sweet to God. [13]

~C.H. Spurgeon (1834-1892)

The man Christ Jesus ... being so near to the Father, and so dear to the Father, and so much in with the Father, can doubtless accomplish anything with the Father, which makes for his glory and our good. [14]

~Thomas Brooks (1608-1680)

O Lord, forgive me [for] _____ (Here, name the sin that most troubles your conscience) .... Reconcile me once again, O merciful Mediator, unto your Father; for though there be nothing in me that can please him, yet I know that in you, and for your sake, he is well pleased. [15]

~Lewis Bayly (c.1575-1631)

† † †

Jesus Always Lives as Our Intercessor

He is able to save to the uttermost those who draw near to God through him, since he always lives to make intercession for them.
(Heb. 7:25)

[We so] little think [of] how busy our Mediator ... is now in heaven for us, ... that Christ is appearing, and his blood is crying, and his prayers are ascending, and his robe of righteousness is covering us. [16]

~Isaac Ambrose (1604-1664)

Labor [then] when you are about to pray, to stir up in your souls the most lively and serious belief of [these] unseen things. [17]

~Richard Baxter (1615-1691)

[By faith, look] to the perpetual intercession of Christ .... O remember that he is not weak, when we are weak .... If you heard Christ pray for you, would it not encourage you to pray? [18]

~Richard Baxter (1615-1691)

Christ is not weary of serving you. When you have done your duties, he takes your persons and duties, and presents all unto his Father; he prays over your prayers, continues praying, and saying, "Lord accept [this] short, poor, imperfect service done on earth, for my sake." [19]

~Isaac Ambrose (1604-1664)

If your weak prayer be once mingled with the glorious and heavenly prayer of Jesus Christ, the weakness will soon vanish, and your prayer will find acceptance with God. [20]

~Isaac Ambrose (1604-1664)

[One may say], "O I am so much opposed that I cannot pray; alas! my prayers are dull, weak, and dry, and without spirit and life." If so, be humbled for it; and yet know this, that when you cannot, Christ prays for you, and he prays that you may pray. [21]

~Isaac Ambrose (1604-1664)

I know of nothing that has so much impressed upon me the sense of the importance of praying at all times and being constantly in prayer as the thought that this is the current main business of my risen Lord. [22]

~R.A. Torrey (1856-1928)

O my soul, rouse up, and set this blessed [truth] before your face! Take a full view of it, until your affections begin to be warm, and you begin to cry, "O for my part in Christ's intercession!" [23]

~Isaac Ambrose (1604-1664)

Lord, I have heard that there is an office erected in heaven, that Christ, as priest, should be ever praying and interceding for his people. O that I may feel the efficacy of Christ's intercession! And now in prayer, O that I could feel in this prayer, the warmth, and heat, and spiritual fire, which usually falls down from Christ's intercession into the heart! Lord, warm my spirit in this duty![24]

~*Isaac Ambrose (1604-1664)*

O my soul, look up, consider Jesus your Savior in these respects! I am persuaded, if you but knew, if you could but see, what a deal of work Christ has in hand, and how he carries it on for your salvation, it would melt your heart into tears of joy! ... O blessed is the man, that knows how to meditate on this day and night![25]

~*Isaac Ambrose (1604-1664)*

He ever lives above
for me to intercede:
His all-redeeming love,
his precious blood to plead:
His blood atoned for every race
and sprinkles now the throne of grace.[26]

~*Charles Wesley (1707-1788)*

[O Lord, help] us to believe ... with full and growing confidence, ... that the feeble prayers which we are now offering are really heard by you and are powerful to obtain for us the help which we need, because we have a High Priest ever living to make intercession for us.[27]

~*Edward Bickersteth (1786-1850)*

✝ ✝ ✝

Jesus Sympathizes as Our High Priest

For we do not have a high priest who is unable to sympathize
with our weaknesses, but one who in every respect has been
tempted as we are, yet without sin.
(Heb. 4:15)

I reveal my grief to my friend. I discern the emotions of his soul, I mark the trembling lip, the sympathizing look, the moistened eye—my friend is touched with my sorrow. But oh, what is this sympathy—tender, soothing, grateful as it is—compared to the sympathy with which the great High Priest in heaven enters into my case, is moved with my grief, is touched with the feeling of my infirmity?[28]

~Octavius Winslow (1808-1878)

From the moment he entered our world [our Lord] became leagued with suffering; he identified himself with it in its almost endless forms. He seemed to have been born with a tear in his eye, with a shade of sadness on his brow. He was prophesied as a man of sorrows and acquainted with grief (Isa. 53:3).... He came to suffer; he came to bear the curse—he came to drain the deep cup of wrath, to weep, to bleed, to die.[29]

~Octavius Winslow (1808-1878)

[Now] Christ in heaven is burning and flaming in compassion towards his weak ones; and therefore, he pleads, intercedes, and prays to God for them.[30]

~Isaac Ambrose (1604-1664)

There is not a moment of time, nor an event of life, nor a circumstance of daily history, nor a mental or spiritual emotion, in which [we] are not borne upon the love, and remembered in the ceaseless intercession of Christ.[31]

~Octavius Winslow (1808-1878)

Tempted ones are peculiarly precious to Jesus. It is his own temptation over again, in the people of his members. And if there be a niche in his heart deeper, warmer, or more sacred than another, it is where he hides and shelters his disciples tempted by Satan and sin. [32]

~Octavius Winslow (1808-1878)

I am often tempted to say, 'How can this Man save us? How can Christ in heaven deliver me from lusts which I feel raging in me, and nets I feel enclosing me?' ... [But] if I could hear Christ praying for me in the next room, I would not fear a million enemies. Yet the distance makes no difference; he is praying for me. [33]

~Robert Murray M'Cheyne (1813-1843)

Simon, Simon, behold, Satan demanded to have you, that he might sift you like wheat, but I have prayed for you that your faith may not fail. (Luke 22:31-32)

As [Christ prayed for] Peter on earth, so doubtless he does in heaven for those who come unto God by him. He takes notice of their case. His eye is always upon them. He sees their fainting faith. He marks their struggles .... He sees when they would fain come to him, and Satan keeps them back or casts them down, or whispers malignant doubts; and seeing all those, he takes their case into his hand and pleads for them with God. [34]

~Horatius Bonar (1808-1889)

Oh, who can fully describe the blessings that flow through the intercession of the Son of God? The love, the sympathy, the forethought, the carefulness, the minute interest in all our concerns, are blessings beyond description. Tried, tempted believer! Jesus makes intercession for you. Your case is not unknown to him. Your sorrow is not hidden from him. Your name is on his heart. Your burden is on his shoulder; and because he not only has prayed for you, but prays for you now, your faith shall not fail. Your great accuser may stand at your right hand to condemn you, but your great Advocate stands at the right hand of God to plead for you. And greater is he that is for you, than all that are against you. [35]

~*Octavius Winslow (1808-1878)*

If God is for us, who can be against us? .... Who is to condemn? Christ Jesus is the one who died—more than that, who was raised—who is at the right hand of God, who indeed is interceding for us. (Rom. 8:31, 34)

Before the throne of God above
I have a strong and perfect plea,
A great High Priest whose name is Love,
Who ever lives and pleads for me.
My name is graven on his hands,
My name is written on his heart;
I know that while in heaven he stands,
No tongue can bid me thence depart. [36]

~*Charitie Lees (Smith) Bancroft (1841-1923)*

When the devil shows the blackness of [our] sins—Christ shows the redness of his wounds! [37]

~*Thomas Watson (1620-1686)*

[Lord], when I look upon my own [prayers]; there is so much deadness, so much hardness of heart, and so many distractions that do accompany them, that I am afraid they will never be accepted. But, O Lord, it is the work of our great High Priest, to take away the weeds of [my prayer], and to present the [prayer]. Now, O Lord, I come unto you as my High Priest. Oh, carry my prayers into the bosom of God the Father. [38]

~*William Bridge (c. 1600-1670)*

† † †

Jesus Opened the Way by His Blood

Therefore, brothers, since we have confidence to enter the holy places
by the blood of Jesus, by the new and living way that he opened for
us through the curtain ... let us draw near. (Heb. 10:19-22)

The way into God's presence is more fully opened by the sacrifice and blood of Jesus than it ever was, even when by vision
or dream or voice God spoke to his saints of old. The blood of
Christ is so powerful, the atonement of the Son of God is so glorious, the intercession of Christ at the right hand of the Father is
so prevailing ... that a man of God coming into his presence by
the blood of the everlasting covenant may enjoy fellowship and
converse with God more close, more filial, more real and holy,
than that which marked Abraham, Isaac, and Jacob. Seek, oh,
seek it, then. Be not content with standing in the outer courts,
when the blood gives you admission into the holiest. [39]

~Octavius Winslow (1808-1878)

Our prayers, how wandering, how wavering they are! When we
get nearest to God, how far off we are! When we are most like
him, how greatly unlike him we are! ... Therefore, keep your
eye on the blood of Jesus, that the sin even of your holy things
may be put away by the sacrifice once offered on Calvary. [40]

~C.H. Spurgeon (1834-1892)

In all true prayer, great stress should be laid on the blood of
Jesus .... Where the atoning blood is kept out of view ... [and]
not made the grand plea, there is a deficiency of power in prayer
.... God has crowned his dearly beloved Son, and he will have us
crown him too; and never do we place a brighter crown upon
his blessed head, than when we plead his finished righteousness
as the ground of our acceptance, and his atoning blood as our
great argument for the bestowment of all blessing with God. [41]

~Octavius Winslow (1808-1878)

Beloved Christian! The blood of Jesus! The blood of the Lamb! Oh think what it means. God gave it for your redemption. God accepted it when his Son entered heaven and presented it on your behalf. God has it forever in his sight as the fruit, the infinitely well-pleasing proof, of his Son's obedience unto death. God points you to it and asks you to believe in the divine satisfaction it gives to him, in its omnipotent energy, in its everlasting sufficiency. Oh, will you not this day believe that that blood gives you, sinful and feeble as you are, liberty, confidence, boldness to draw nigh, to enter the very Holiest?[42]

~Andrew Murray (1828-1917)

I do behold you, Lord, by faith, even now standing with the blood of the covenant in your hand, and presenting me, even me, poor, wretched, worthless me, as one of [those purchased by] this blood.[43]

~Robert Hawker (1753-1827)

Come, friends, fall down on your knees, and confess your sins as having merited hell and damnation; but since God has held forth Christ to be a propitiation for sin, tell the Lord how much you need him, humbly address him with tears in your eyes and sorrow in your hearts, after this manner: "Lord, I am among the fallen sons of Adam, ... having added to the first sin many thousands of actual transgressions. Every sin deserves your wrath and curse, I deserve damnation; but my case is not like that of the fallen angels, you have sent your only well-beloved Son to redeem lost mankind, he interposed [between] flaming wrath and guilty sinners, he endured that which would have sunk sinners eternally into torments, and I hear he is at your right hand to intercede for sinners. I am a miserable, helpless, [and] hopeless sinner, ... but you bid all welcome that come to you in his name. He has successfully managed this work of mediation, and carried thousands of souls to heaven, whose case was as forlorn as mine. O give me Christ or else I die; give me Christ and I shall live."[44]

~Oliver Heywood (1630-1702)

[Father], you offer your dear, sweet, heavenly Son, the Lord Jesus Christ, unto my soul. O my God, I accept him. You [offer] his blood unto me. Lord, I receive it with both hands [and] with all my heart …. To him I go that he would undertake the cure of my miserable soul. [45]

~Cotton Mather (1663-1728)

† † †

Let Us Draw Near through the Son

Let us then with confidence draw near to the throne of grace, that we may receive mercy and find grace to help in time of need. (Heb. 4:16)

Go to the Lord in your worst frames; stay not from him until you get a good one. Satan's grand argument to keep a soul from prayer is, "Go not with that cold and insensible frame; go not with that hard and sinful heart; stay until you are more fit to approach God." … But the Gospel says, "Go in your very worst frames." Christ says, "Come just as you are." [46]

~Octavius Winslow (1808-1878)

When I have sinned, and come creeping up to my closet with a guilty conscience and an aching heart, and feel that I am not worthy to be called God's son, I still have an advocate! … "If any man sin we have an advocate [with the Father]" (1 John 2:2). Oh! my soul, there is the music of God's heart in those words. [47]

~C.H. Spurgeon (1834-1892)

I stand before him in my filth, in my weakness, with conscience gnawing at me in the sense of many infirmities, many a sin and shortcoming and omission. [Yet from the throne of grace comes the] tender love from God's heart to me, and I get for all my weakness and sin, pity and pardon, and find mercy [from] the Lord in that day. [48]

~Alexander Maclaren (1826-1910)

To the dear fountain of thy blood, Incarnate God, I fly;
Here let me wash my sinful soul from crimes of deepest dye

A guilty, weak, and helpless worm, on thy kind arms I fall;
Be thou my strength and righteousness, my Jesus, and my all. [49]

~Isaac Watts (1674-1748)

I felt such delight in asking [God] to look on me in Jesus, not to look at me at all, except in his beloved Son; for then, and only then, he can say, "You are all fair, my love, there is no spot in you" (Song 4:7). It is blessed, when you feel very vile, to hide in Jesus, and though still as vile as ever in yourself, to say, "Abba, Father!" [50]

~Anonymous (1852)

Depth of mercy! Can there be mercy still reserved for me?
Can my God his wrath forbear? Me the chief of sinners, spare?

I have long withstood his grace: long provoked him to his face;
Would not hearken to his calls; grieved him by a thousand falls ....

There for me the Savior stands, shows his wounds and spreads his hands:
God is love! I know, I feel; Jesus weeps, but loves me still! [51]

~Charles Wesley (1707-1788)

Who has not experienced it? ... How often has guilt caused the head to hang down, and a sense of utter vileness and worthlessness covered the soul with shame! ... Then does the blessed Spirit ... unfold Jesus to the soul as being all that it needs to give it full, free and near access to God. He removes the eye from self, and fixes and fastens it upon the blood that pleads louder for mercy than all [our] sins can plead for condemnation.[52]

~*Octavius Winslow (1808-1878)*

For every look at yourself, take ten looks at Christ. He is altogether lovely. Such infinite majesty, and yet such meekness and grace, and all for sinners, even the chief! Live much in the smiles of God. Bask in his beams. Feel his all-seeing eye settled on you in love, and [recline] in his almighty arms.[53]

~*Robert Murray M'Cheyne (1813-1843)*

Approach, my soul, the mercy seat where Jesus answers prayer; there humbly fall before his feet, for none can perish there ....

Bowed down beneath a load of sin, by Satan sorely pressed, by war without and fears within, I come to thee for rest.

Be thou my shield and hiding place, that, sheltered near thy side, I may my fierce accuser face, and tell him thou hast died.

O wondrous love! to bleed and die, to bear the cross and shame, that guilty sinners, such as I, might plead thy gracious name![54]

~*John Newton (1725-1807)*

Pray on, dear saint! ... Your words may be few—your utterances stammering—your faith weak—yet pray on. God having accepted you in the Person of Jesus, will on the ground of his worthiness, accept the sweet savor of your prayers.[55]

~*Octavius Winslow (1808-1878)*

O LORD, I call upon you ... Let my prayer be counted as incense before you. (Psa. 141:1-2)

Great High Priest, ever pleading at God's right hand, receive our sin-soiled prayers, cleanse them in your precious blood, perfume them by the sweet savor of your merits, and obtain acceptance for them. Extend your wounded hands in our behalf.[56]

~*Henry Law (1797-1884)*

Seven

Praying in the Spirit

We Cannot Pray Without the Holy Spirit

Praying in the Holy Spirit. † *Praying at all times in the Spirit.*
(Jude 20; Eph. 6:18)

Prayer is the creation of the Holy Spirit! We cannot do without prayer and we cannot pray without the Holy Spirit![1]

~*C.H. Spurgeon (1834-1892)*

The Holy Spirit has been, in a great measure, so long departed from his churches, that we are tempted to think that all his operations in exhortations, in prayer and preaching, belong only to the first age of Christianity.... [But] since in many Scriptures the Spirit of God is promised to be given us, to dwell in us, and to be in us, and to assist in prayer; why should we industriously exclude him?[2]

~*Isaac Watts (1674-1748)*

Look at a ship without a wind, becalmed in the middle sea, its sails flapping idly hither and thither; what a difference from the same ship when the wind has filled its sails, and it is making joyful progress to the haven whither it is bound! The Breath of

God, *that* is the wind which must fill the sails of our souls. We must pray in the Spirit ... if we would pray at all.[3]

~*R. C. Trench (1807-1886)*

The believer should [consider] the true character of his prayers. Are they lively and spiritual? Are they the exercises of the heart, or of the understanding merely? Are they the breathings of the indwelling Spirit, or the cold observance of a form without the power?[4]

~*Octavius Winslow (1808-1878)*

My dear friends, may I put the question to you? Will you try to answer it honestly? Have you prayed in the Holy Spirit? ... The preacher standing here begs God to search him in [this] matter.[5]

~*C.H. Spurgeon (1834-1892)*

O Lord, what we most of all need ... is that you should give to us your own Spirit to make intercession in us and for us. We implore this gift from you. Without your Spirit our prayers [are] cold, formal, full of vanities, distractions, and hypocrisies—a deception before man and a mockery before God. But only give us your Spirit, and we shall rise beyond the encumbrance of the flesh and the weakness of the spiritual man, and as on eagles' wings mount up to you, thirsting after you, and delighting in you, and worshiping you in spirit and in truth.[6]

~*Edward Bickersteth (1786-1850)*

† † †

The Spirit is Given to Those Who Ask

If you then, who are evil, know how to give good gifts to your children, how much more will the heavenly Father give the Holy Spirit to those who ask him! (Luke 11:13)

We are taught in a special manner to pray that God would give his Holy Spirit unto us.[7]

~John Owen (1616-1683)

What is the most eminent thing, the best [thing, Christ] would direct you to pray for? Though he had given the particulars in the Lord's Prayer (Luke 11:1-4), he singles out this [gift] of the Spirit. (Luke 11:13)[8]

~Thomas Goodwin (1600-1680)

After Christ had answered the request of his disciples, and taught them how to pray, by giving them a pattern of prayer, he recommends them to ask his Father for the Holy Spirit, in order to [have] a fuller and further assistance and instruction in this work of prayer.[9]

~Isaac Watts (1674-1748)

Let us ask Father to give the Holy Spirit to us! Let us ask him to be in us more and more mightily as the Spirit of prayer![10]

~C.H. Spurgeon (1834-1892)

[Let us] pray for the Spirit, that is, for more of him, though God has endued [us] with him already.[11]

~John Bunyan (1628-1688)

May we [realize that we are the] very temples of [the Holy Spirit's] perpetual indwelling, and [may] his graces wholly replenish our souls. As the *sun* is full of light, as the *ocean* is full of drops, as the *heavens* are full of glory—so may we be filled with his presence![12]

~Henry Law (1797-1884)

Pray for the Spirit above all [and] bless God for this Holy Spirit as one of the greatest blessings of all …. For when God gives you [the Spirit] more and more to dwell in you, and fill you, and mingle with your heart, he brings with himself all [other needful things].[13]

~Thomas Goodwin (1600-1680)

I was stirred up to pray for the Spirit ... because I felt an absence of the Spirit exceedingly much ... and acted by my own spirit in everything. However, I felt a little of God's Spirit smoking forth in some weak desires after him …. [One] great hindrance for me in getting this Spirit [is that] I content myself with a little measure of him.[14]

~*Thomas Shepard (1605-1649)*

If you do not feel the Holy Spirit at work distinctly and perceptibly, even now, then lift your heart to God for him.[15]

~*C.H. Spurgeon (1834-1892)*

Come to God ... desiring to be filled with the fullness of the Spirit, and the sense of [your] own emptiness will [compel your] prayer.[16]

~*Richard Sibbes (1577-1635)*

[O Lord], we are blind in our own understandings; enlighten us. We are perplexed; set us right. We are dull; quicken us. We are empty; fill us. We are dark; shine upon us. We are ready to go out of the way; establish us …. The best that we can bring to you is emptiness. Therefore do good to us; fill us with your fullness …. Give us first your grace, your Spirit, which is the Spring of all good things.[17]

~*Richard Sibbes (1577-1635)*

[O Lord], you have said, if we being evil, know how to give good gifts unto our children, much more will you give your Holy Spirit to them that ask you; we ask [for him], O heavenly Father …. We are weak and sinful, and want to bring forth love, joy, peace, long-suffering, gentleness, goodness, faith, meekness, temperance, and all the blessed fruits of the Spirit; give us then your Spirit.[18]

~*Edward Bickersteth (1786-1850)*

† † †

The Spirit Helps Us in Our Weakness

Likewise the Spirit helps us in our weakness. For we do not know what to pray for as we ought. (Rom. 8:26a)

If left to himself, [the Christian] does not know how to pray, or how he ought to pray, [but] God has come down to meet us in this helplessness of ours by giving us the Holy Spirit himself. [19]

~Andrew Murray (1828-1917)

It is true, that whatever we ought to pray for is declared in the Scripture, yes, and [directly] comprised in the Lord's Prayer; but it is one thing to have what we ought to pray for *in the book*, [and] another thing to have it *in our minds and hearts* .... [And] it is out of the abundance of the heart that the mouth must speak in [prayer]. (Matt. 12:34) [20]

~John Owen (1616-1683)

I am often afraid for myself as a minister that I pray too easily. I have been praying for these forty or fifty years and it becomes, as far as man is concerned, an easy thing to pray. We all have been taught to pray, and when we are called upon, we can pray, ... [but] I am afraid we think we are praying often when there is little real prayer. [21]

~Andrew Murray (1828-1917)

[O Lord], we feel how easy it is to bow the head and cover the face, and yet the thoughts may be all astray, and the mind may be wandering hither and thither, so that there shall be no real prayer at all. Come, Holy Spirit, help us to feel that we are in the immediate presence of God. [22]

~C.H. Spurgeon (1834-1892)

When you go to prayer, be impressed with a sense of your inability to manage it aright. [23]

~*Thomas Boston (1676-1732)*

When you go to prayer, be convinced of your absolute need of the Spirit. Look for him ... and lay yourselves open to his influences. Labor to revive that conviction at every occasion of prayer, and keep it up throughout. [24]

~*Thomas Boston (1676-1732)*

The Holy Spirit could pray a hundred-fold more in us if we were only conscious of our ignorance, because we would then feel our dependence upon him. [25]

~*Andrew Murray (1828-1917)*

It is good to confide in him, to confess that you would but cannot pray, that your desires are languid and your love cool, that the lips which should be touched with fire are frostbitten, that the wings which ought to have borne you to heaven are clipped. He understands and loves to be appealed to and will assuredly quicken the flagging soul until it shall mount up as on eagle wings, running without wearying and walking without faintness. [26]

~*F.B. Meyer (1847-1929)*

Never do we feel [our infirmities] more than at the hour of prayer. Sometimes our thoughts scatter like a flock of sheep, or flag and faint before the spiritual effort of stirring ourselves up to take hold on God .... [Yet] in all this the Spirit helps us. [27]

~*F.B. Meyer (1847-1929)*

It is widely known to those who are in any way exercised in [prayer], what difficulties lie in the way of its due performance, what discouragements rise up against it, ... what aversion there is to it in our corrupted nature, and what distractions and weariness are apt to befall us under it .... [Yet] this gift of the Spirit of grace and supplication is given to us by Jesus Christ to relieve us against all these things, to help our infirmities, to give us free-dom, liberty, and confidence in our approaches to the throne of grace.²⁸

~John Owen (1616-1683)

[One may say], "How can I pray? My mind wanders: I chatter like a crane; I roar like a beast in pain; I moan in the brokenness of my heart, but oh, my God, I know not what it is my inmost spirit needs; or if I know it, I know not how to frame my pe-tition aright before you. I know not how to open my lips in your majestic presence: I am so troubled that I cannot speak. My spiritual distress robs me of the power to pour out my heart before my God." Now, beloved, it is in such a plight as this that the Holy Spirit aids us with his divine help, and hence he is a very present help in time of trouble.²⁹

~C.H. Spurgeon (1834-1892)

Lord, I am low, flat, and unfeeling; send the powerful arm of your blessed Holy Spirit to work all his gracious dispositions in me and raise up my affections to you …. Send your Spirit to fetch in my roaming and wandering heart …. Let your Spirit scatter these mists of ignorance, and drive away these flies of distracting thoughts, so that my heart may be with you, and what I am presenting may be a sweet savor unto [you].³⁰

~Oliver Heywood (1630-1702)

Come, Holy Spirit, Heavenly Dove, with all thy quickening powers;
Kindle a flame of sacred love in these cold hearts of ours.

Look, how we grovel here below, fond of these trifling toys;
Our souls, can neither fly nor go, to reach eternal joys.

In vain we tune our formal songs, in vain we strive to rise;
Hosannas languish on our tongues, and our devotion dies.

Dear Lord, and shall we ever live at this poor dying rate,
Our love so faint, so cold to thee, and thine to us so great?

Come, Holy Spirit, Heavenly Dove, with all thy quickening
powers;
Come, shed abroad a Savior's love, and that shall kindle ours. [31]

~*Isaac Watts (1674-1748)*

† † †

The Spirit Stimulates and Sustains
Our Prayers

It is the Spirit who gives life; the flesh is no help at all. (John 6:63)

True prayer is from the indwelling Spirit. It is he that wakes
up prayer in us, both as to its matter and its manner. We know
not what or how to pray. He alone can teach us both; and he
does this by coming into us, and filling our whole being with
himself. [32]

~*Horatius Bonar (1808-1889)*

The truth is, Christian, you will but bungle at [prayer] without
this help of God's Spirit …. Do not think you can wrestle out
the business yourself. [33]

~*Oliver Heywood (1630-1702)*

The Holy Spirit is absolutely necessary to make everything that
we do to be alive …. We can pray as machines … [and] shall do
so unless the Spirit of God is with us! [34]

~*C.H. Spurgeon (1834-1892)*

[Though we] always have the Spirit dwelling in [us] as a Spirit of
life, yet [we] cannot pray aright without actual influence from
him. [35]

~*Thomas Boston (1676-1732)*

The Spirit inclines our hearts to pray, and keeps them intent upon the work …. It is only the Spirit of God that … excites us to take occasion from the several concerns of our souls, or from the affairs of life, to go to the mercy-seat, and to abide there …. By his good motions he overcomes our delay, and answers the carnal objections of our sinful and slothful hearts.[36]

~Isaac Watts (1674-1748)

It is the Holy Spirit that holds us to the duty, in opposition to all discouragements, and makes us wrestle and strive with God in prayer, pour out our hearts before him, and stir up ourselves to take hold of him. (cf. Gen. 32:24; Rom. 15:30; Psa. 62:8; Isa. 64:7)[37]

~Isaac Watts (1674-1748)

The Holy Spirit has a wonderful power over renewed hearts, as much power as the skillful minstrel has over the strings among which he lays his accustomed hand, … creating and inspiring sweet notes of gratitude and tones of desire, to which we should have been strangers if it had not been for his divine visitation. He can arouse us from our lethargy, he can warm us out of our lukewarmness, he can enable us when we are on our knees to rise above the ordinary routine of prayer.[38]

~C.H. Spurgeon (1834-1892)

It is important, however, that we make no mistake about the intercession of the Spirit. We are not to defer all our prayers until we have some special inward impression to pray for each particular object, or some deep and vivid emotion respecting it. The Holy Spirit may [guide] us through the ordinary times and habits of prayer …. We must trust his help and believe that we receive it even when we have no special internal impressions.[39]

~A.B. Simpson (1843-1919)

Though the Spirit of God should sometimes withdraw himself in his influences, yet my duty and obligation to [be constant in] prayer still remains. (Rom. 12:12)[40]

~Isaac Watts (1674-1748)

[Therefore], ask for the Spirit, expect his influence, be diligent, and although you [may not] actually observe his workings, you may [still] reckon upon it, that even while you may suppose yourselves to have been passed by, the Spirit is already cooperating with your first feeble endeavors. [41]

~*Andrew Murray (1828-1917)*

O Holy Spirit, the intercessor to help our infirmities in prayer, grant us your aid that we may pray in the Holy Spirit: with all that faith and humility, that contrition and earnestness, and that glowing desire and love, which are the fruit of your grace. Do enable us to offer up the fervent and effectual prayer that avails much. [42]

~*Edward Bickersteth (1786-1850)*

† † †

The Spirit Prays for Us and Cooperates with Our Praying

… the Spirit of adoption as sons, by whom we cry. … the Spirit himself intercedes for us. (Rom. 8:15; 26)

So entirely does the Spirit identify himself with us, that our desires are reckoned his, and his desires ours. He not only helps our infirmities, but he comes into us, unites himself, as it were, to us, makes himself one with us; fills us, joins his desires to ours, his voice to ours, his cries to ours, so that they both come up as one before God. [43]

~*Horatius Bonar (1808-1889)*

There is a concurrence both of the Spirit of God and the … spirit of the Christian [during prayer]. Hence, we find both the Holy

Spirit is said to pray *in us* (Rom. 8:26), and we [are] said to pray *in him*. (Jude 20)[44]

~*William Gurnall (1616-1679)*

While in one passage [the Apostle] says that *we* cry out in the Holy Spirit, "Abba, Father" (Rom. 8:15), in another passage again he says, God has sent the *Spirit of his Son* into your hearts, crying, "Abba, Father" (Gal. 4:6).[45]

~*Augustine of Hippo (354-430)*

[There is] a wonderful blending of divine and human cooperation in prayer![46]

~*Andrew Murray (1828-1917)*

And he that searches the hearts knows what is the mind of the Spirit, because he makes intercession for the saints according to the will of God. (Rom. 8:27)

Our Father in heaven ... is essentially acquainted with all the [dictations] and breathings of the Spirit in the heart .... He knows the mind of the Spirit in his saints. Oh [what a] sweet encouragement to prayer![47]

~*Octavius Winslow (1808-1878)*

[The Spirit infuses] himself into each petition, so that *he* becomes the petitioner, the pleader. Thus he pleads both *for* us and *in* us. He throws himself into our case; he seizes hold of us in our weakness; he bears us up as one who has come to our help; he drowns our cries in his, so that God hears.[48]

~*Horatius Bonar (1808-1889)*

As the Spirit of God does excite the Christian's affections, so he *regulates and directs them* .... We, alas! are prone to overbend the bow in some petitions, and [lack] strength to bend it enough in some others. One while we overshoot the butt, praying absolutely for that which we should ask conditionally; another time we shoot beside the mark, either by praying for what God has not promised, or too selfishly that which is promised. Now the Spirit helps the Christian's infirmity in this respect, for he makes intercession for the saints according to the will of God (Rom. 8:27), that is, he so holds the reins of their affections and directs them, that they keep their right way and due order, not flying out to unwarrantable heats and inordinate desires. He, by his secret whispers, instructs them when to let out their affections full speed, and when to take them up again. [49]

~William Gurnall (1616-1679)

Put yourself into the hands of the Spirit, for prayer and everything else. ... Pray in the Spirit. Delight in prayer. Cherish the Spirit's groans. [50]

~Horatius Bonar (1808-1889)

O divine Advocate, teach us to know the priceless value of your intercessions! [51]

~A.J. Gordon (1836-1895)

[O Lord], fill us with all the fullness of God. Make our bodies the temples of your Holy Spirit. Consecrate all our lives as a living sacrifice on your altar. May your Spirit now and evermore ... move in every movement of our minds. [52]

~Henry Law (1797-1884)

† † †

The Spirit Prays with Groanings

But the Spirit himself intercedes for us with groanings too deep for words. (Rom. 8:26b)

True prayer often takes the form of groans. The longings produced in us by the indwelling Spirit are such as cannot get vent to themselves in words …. We try to pray; our hearts are too full; we cannot; we break down; it may be with sorrow, or ignorance, or the intensity of our feelings, or the soreness of our trials, or the multitude of our longings. Yes, we break down before God; we become dumb; we can only groan. But the groan is true prayer …. For thus we groan with the rest of a groaning creation (Rom. 8:22-23); and all these groans are at length to be heard and fully answered. [53]

~Horatius Bonar (1808-1889)

When you get upstairs into your chamber this evening to pray, and find you cannot pray, but have to moan out, "Lord, I am too full of anguish and too perplexed to pray, hear the voice of my roaring," though you reach to nothing else, you will be really praying …. The sighing of a true heart is infinitely more acceptable [than all fine language], for it is the work of the Spirit of God. [54]

~C.H. Spurgeon (1834-1892)

I cry aloud to God, aloud to God, and he will hear me …. When I remember God, I moan; when I meditate, my spirit faints …. I am so troubled that I cannot speak. (Psa. 77:1-4)

I am feeble and crushed; I groan because of the tumult of my heart. O Lord, all my longing is before you; my sighing is not hidden from you. (Psa. 38:8-9)

God hears [the groanings in the heart]—Jesus understands them—the Spirit creates them—and not one shall be uttered in vain. Whether it be the groaning from a pressure of sin, or from a sense of desire, or from a conviction of need, or from the smiting hand of God himself, that groaning ascends to heaven. [55]

~Octavius Winslow (1808-1878)

I pray you never think lightly of the supplications of your anguish …. That which is thrown up from the depth of the soul,

when it is stirred with a terrible tempest, is more precious than
pearl or coral. [56]

~*C.H. Spurgeon (1834-1892)*

Lord, you know the groanings of our heart; our prayers cannot
express them but we bless you that there is One who makes intercession for us with groanings that cannot be uttered, who is
with us, and dwells in us, and is promised to be with us forever. [57]

~*C.H. Spurgeon (1834-1892)*

† † †

The Spirit Leads Us Through the Word

Understand what the will of the Lord is .... Be filled with the Spirit.
† Let the word of Christ dwell in you richly. (Eph. 5:17-18; Col. 3:16)

As a teaching Spirit ... he enlightens our minds, and helps our
ignorance as to the matter and manner of prayer. [58]

~*Thomas Boston (1676-1732)*

The word is the instrument whereby the Holy Spirit reveals
unto us our wants, when we know not what to ask; and so, he
enables us to make intercessions according to the mind of God.
(Rom. 8:26-27) [59]

~*John Owen (1616-1683)*

The Bible is a noble guide for prayer, both for the matter and
manner thereof; and if we diligently study it, we will not be in
hazard of uttering anything contrary to or inconsistent with it. [60]

~*Thomas Boston (1676-1732)*

The person who wants to pray in the Spirit must meditate much
upon the word so the Holy Spirit can have something through
which he can work .... If we would feed the fire of our prayers

with the fuel of God's word, [many of] our difficulties in prayer would disappear. [61]

~R.A. Torrey (1856-1928)

But the Helper, the Holy Spirit, whom the Father will send in my name, he will teach you all things and bring to your remembrance all that I have said to you. (John 14:26)

The Spirit of God, in praying and preaching, will often bless the use of his own language ... by suggesting to us particular passages of Scripture that are useful to furnish us both with matter and expression in prayer. [62]

~Isaac Watts (1674-1748)

[Indeed], who is it that, almost at any time reading the Scripture with a due reverence for God, and a subjection of his conscience to him, does not have some particular matter of prayer or praise effectually suggested unto him? And Christians would find [great] advantage ... if they would frequently, if not constantly, turn what they read into prayer or praise unto God. [63]

~John Owen (1616-1683)

Come, Holy Spirit, ... we bless you for your holy Scriptures. We receive each word as given directly by your inspiration. In your light may we see light. Shine upon the sacred page. Instruct us in the glorious meaning. Write the transforming gospel on our hearts. [64]

~Henry Law (1797-1884)

† † †

The Spirit Leads Us to the Father and the Son

You have received the Spirit of adoption as sons, by whom we cry,
"Abba! Father!" The Spirit himself bears witness with our spirit that
we are children of God. (Rom. 8:15-16)

[The Spirit] encourages and emboldens us to come to God as a father. This is one main thing twice mentioned in Scripture (Rom. 8:15 and Gal. 4:6). A great part of the life and comfort of prayer consists in coming to God as a reconciled father ... with child-like confidence and child-like reverence. [65]

~Thomas Manton (1620-1677)

The Spirit intercedes for us not in many words or long prayers, but with groanings, with little sounds like "Abba." Small as this word is, it says ever so much. It says: "My Father, I am in great trouble and you seem so far away. But I know I am your child, because you are my Father for Christ's sake. I am loved by you because of the Beloved." [66]

~Martin Luther (1483-1546)

[Satan] tempts you to [think] that God is not your Father,... [but] the Spirit of God is sent on purpose into our hearts for this very work .... Indeed if the Spirit of God did not constantly thus keep up a filial frame, every new failing would cast us back into a mere darkness and confusion. [67]

~Anthony Burgess (1600-1663)

The law scolds us, sin screams at us, death thunders at us, the devil roars at us. In the midst of the clamor the Spirit of Christ cries in our hearts: "Abba, Father." And this little cry of the Spirit transcends [all] the hullabaloo .... Let the law, sin, and the devil cry out against us until their outcry fills heaven and earth.

The Spirit of God outcries them all. Our feeble groans, "Abba, Father," will be heard of God sooner than the combined racket of hell, sin, and the law. [68]

~Martin Luther (1483-1546)

O heavenly Father, give unto us more and more of the Spirit of adoption, that we may look to you as our Father, and cry, "Abba, Father," [with] entire confidence of heart in you. [69]

~Edward Bickersteth (1786-1850)

It is [also] the work of the Holy Spirit in prayer to keep the souls of believers intent upon Jesus Christ. [70]

~John Owen (1616-1683)

The Holy Spirit will, in prayer, constantly remind us of Christ and of his blood and name, as the sure ground of our being heard. [71]

~Andrew Murray (1828-1917)

When the Spirit of truth comes, he will guide you into all the truth .... He will glorify me, for he will take what is mine and declare it to you. (John 16:13-14)

[The Holy Spirit] does many things, but this is what he aims at in all of them, to glorify Christ. Brothers and sisters, what the Holy Spirit does must be right for us to imitate .... Then [let this be] your continual prayer, "Blessed Spirit, help me to always glorify the Lord Jesus Christ!" [72]

~C.H. Spurgeon (1834-1892)

Oh [how the Spirit] longs to draw your attention to Jesus, that you may be forced to cry, "There is beauty in him that I should desire him." [73]

~Horatius Bonar (1808-1889)

[O Father], may your Spirit take of the things of Christ, and show them to us .... Especially reveal to us the wonders of his dying love, and all the glorious issues of the stupendous sacrifice made by his death for our sins. [74]

~*Edward Bickersteth (1786-1850)*

Blessed and Eternal Spirit! Divine Interpreter of Christ! Revealer of Jesus! Lead me into all truth concerning him. Reveal his glory, unveil his beauty, disclose his love, interpret his language, and unfold and apply his truths to my soul. [75]

~*Octavius Winslow (1808-1878)*

† † †

Let Us Walk in the Spirit and Pray in the Spirit

If we live by the Spirit, let us also keep in step with the Spirit.
† *Praying at all times in the Spirit, with all prayer and supplication.*
(Gal 5:25; Eph. 6:18)

Is it not clear that everything in prayer depends upon our trusting the Holy Spirit to do his work in us; yielding ourselves to his leading, depending only and wholly on him? [76]

~*Andrew Murray (1828-1917)*

If we have at all desired or resolved to pray more, let us turn to the very Source of all power and blessing—let us believe that the Spirit of prayer, even in his fullness, is for us. [77]

~*Andrew Murray (1828-1917)*

There is [no one] in the world so great and sweet a friend [who] will do us so much good as the Spirit, if we give him [accommodation]. [78]

~*Richard Sibbes (1577-1635)*

[Therefore], grieve not [the Spirit], ... [but] deal kindly with him when he comes to make a visit of conviction to your consciences to direct and incline you even to difficult and self-denying duties. Live in the Spirit, walk in the Spirit, and then you shall also pray in the Spirit. [79]

~Isaac Watts (1674-1748)

May we never ... quench the Spirit, never resist the Holy Spirit, never grieve the Holy Spirit. But may we pray in the Holy Spirit, and worship God in the Spirit, and be led by the Spirit, and be filled with the Spirit. [80]

~William Jay (1769-1853)

The Spirit of supplication increases in my heart daily. May he increase more and more .... Lord enlarge my narrow heart. [81]

~George Whitefield (1714-1770)

Come, Holy Spirit, we do know you, [for] you have often overshadowed us. Come [now] more fully and take possession of us .... Take our heart, our head, our hands, our feet, and use us. [82]

~C.H. Spurgeon (1834-1892)

O Lord, may we now be filled to the full with [your] Spirit of grace and supplication. In public and in private, in the sanctuary and in the closet, may our life be steeped in prayer. [83]

~Henry Law (1797-1884)

Are you moved to pray? While you muse does the fire burn? ... Oh, then, rise and pray—the Spirit prompts you—the Savior invites you—your heavenly Father waits to answer you. [84]

~Octavius Winslow (1808-1878)

Epilogue

Finally, be strong in the Lord and in the strength of his might....
praying at all times in the Spirit, with all prayer and supplication. To
that end, keep alert with all perseverance (Eph. 6:10, 18).

The one concern of the devil is to keep Christians from praying. He fears nothing from prayerless studies, prayerless work and prayerless religion. He laughs at our toil, mocks at our wisdom, but trembles when we pray.[1]

~Samuel Chadwick (1860-1932)

If there were not a kind of omnipotency in [prayer], if it were not able to do wonders in heaven, and wonders on earth, and wonders in the hearts and lives and ways of men—Satan would never have such an aching tooth against it as he has.[2]

~Thomas Brooks (1608-1680)

Satan has such an impression of dread upon him—from the remembrance of what he has suffered from the hands of prayer—that he will turn every stone, and try every way, to obstruct you in it .... Satan cannot deny but great wonders have been wrought by prayer. As the spirit of prayer goes up, so his kingdom goes down.[3]

~William Gurnall (1616-1679)

The devil is aware that one hour of close fellowship, hearty converse with God in prayer is able to pull down what he has been contriving and building many a year.[4]

~John Flavel (c.1627-1691)

Satan works to become master of the Christian's inner chamber, because he knows that if there has been unfaithfulness in prayer, the testimony will not bring much loss to his kingdom.[5]

~*Andrew Murray (1828-1917)*

We shall not find it easy to pray, or maintain the spirit of prayer, for experience teaches us the truth of words, ... "Satan strikes ever at the root of faith or at the root of diligence."[6]

~*Gordon Watt (1865-1928)*

[The devil] employs every artifice to create a spirit of carelessness in regard to prayer, and to tempt a substitution of work for spiritual devotion. For in the satanic survey of the believer's activities, well does the evil one know that Christian endeavor with little prayer need not cause him great concern.[7]

~*Gordon Watt (1865-1928)*

It was a masterstroke of the devil when he got the Church and the ministry so generally to lay aside the mighty weapon of prayer. The devil is perfectly willing that the Church should multiply its organizations ... if it will only give up praying .... But when men and women arise who believe in prayer, and who pray in the way the Bible teaches us to pray, prayer accomplishes as much as it ever did.[8]

~*R.A. Torrey (1856-1928)*

[This] great living question has been considered by many, "Will we really be determined to win back again the weapon of believing prayer that Satan has, in a measure, taken away from us?" Let us set before ourselves the serious importance of this conflict.[9]

~*Andrew Murray (1828-1917)*

In war, everything depends on each soldier being obedient to the word of command, even though it may cost him his life. In our strife with Satan, we will not conquer unless each one of us holds himself ready, even in the reading of this simple book, to say from the heart, "What God says, I will do; and if I see that anything is according to his will, I will immediately receive it and act upon it."[10]

~*Andrew Murray (1828-1917)*

I have asked the Lord that he would give this book a place in some inner chambers, and that he may assist the reader, so that, as he sees what God's will is, he may immediately give himself up to doing it.[11]

~*Andrew Murray (1828-1917)*

Get alone and pray over this book, and for its unworthy sinful author. ... And let our prayers continue to meet daily at the throne of grace until our souls meet before the throne of God.[12]

~*Oliver Heywood (1630-1702)*

I shall, by assisting grace, follow this poor piece with my prayers, that it may be so blessed from on high, as that it may work mightily to the internal and eternal welfare—both of reader, hearer, and writer.[13]

~*Thomas Brooks (1608-1680)*

May the grace of the Lord Jesus Christ and the love of God and the fellowship of the Holy Spirit be with us all. Amen.

Jesus' Example of Prayer

(In this section, italics signify the prayers of Jesus)

† † †

Jesus Prayed in Communion
with His Father

Mark 1:35—And rising very early in the morning, while it was still dark, he departed and went out to a desolate place, and there he prayed.

Luke 6:12-13—In these days he went out to the mountain to pray, and all night he continued in prayer to God. And when day came, he called his disciples and chose from them twelve, whom he named apostles.

Mark 6:45-47—Immediately he made his disciples get into the boat and go before him to the other side, to Bethsaida, while he dismissed the crowd. And after he had taken leave of them, he went up on the mountain to pray. And when evening came, the boat was out on the sea, and he was alone on the land.

Luke 9:18—Now it happened that as he was praying alone, the disciples were with him. And he asked them, "Who do the crowds say that I am?"

Luke 9:28-29—Now about eight days after these sayings he

took with him Peter and John and James and went up on the mountain to pray. And as he was praying, the appearance of his face was altered, and his clothing became dazzling white.

Luke 11:1 — Now Jesus was praying in a certain place, and when he finished, one of his disciples said to him, "Lord, teach us to pray, as John taught his disciples."

† † †

Jesus Prayed with Thanksgiving to the Father

Matthew 11:25-26 — *"I thank you, Father, Lord of heaven and earth, that you have hidden these things from the wise and understanding and revealed them to little children; yes, Father, for such was your gracious will."*

Luke 9:16 — And taking the five loaves and the two fish, he looked up to heaven and said a blessing over them.

John 6:11 — Jesus then took the loaves, and when he had given thanks, he distributed them to those who were seated. So also the fish, as much as they wanted.

John 11:41-42 — And Jesus lifted up his eyes and said, *"Father, I thank you that you have heard me. I knew that you always hear me, but I said this on account of the people standing around, that they may believe that you sent me."*

Mark 14:22-23 — And as they were eating, he took bread, and after blessing it he broke it and gave it to them, and said, "Take; this is my body." And he took a cup, and when he had given thanks he gave it to them, and they all drank of it.

Luke 24:30-31 — When he was at table with them, he took the

bread and blessed and broke it and gave it to them. And their eyes were opened, and they recognized him. And he vanished from their sight.

† † †

Jesus Prayed with Supplication and Consecration to the Father

Luke 3:21-22—Now when all the people were baptized, and when Jesus also had been baptized and was praying, the heavens were opened, and the Holy Spirit descended on him in bodily form, like a dove; and a voice came from heaven, "You are my beloved Son; with you I am well pleased."

John 12:27-28— *"Now is my soul troubled. And what shall I say? 'Father, save me from this hour'? But for this purpose I have come to this hour. Father, glorify your name."* Then a voice came from heaven: "I have glorified it, and I will glorify it again."

John 17:1, 6, 19-20, 26—When Jesus had spoken these words, he lifted up his eyes to heaven, and said, *"Father, the hour has come; glorify your Son that the Son may glorify you .... I have manifested your name to the people whom you gave me out of the world .... And for their sake I consecrate myself, that they also may be sanctified in truth. I do not ask for these only, but also for those who will believe in me through their word .... I made known to them your name, and I will continue to make it known, that the love with which you have loved me may be in them, and I in them."*

Mark 14:35-36—And going a little farther, he fell on the ground and prayed that, if it were possible, the hour might pass from him. And he said, *"Abba, Father, all things are possible for you.*

Remove this cup from me. Yet not what I will, but what you will."

Matthew 27: 46; Luke 23:46—And about the ninth hour Jesus cried out with a loud voice, saying, *"Eli, Eli, lema sabachthani?"* that is, *"My God, my God, why have you forsaken me?"* ... Then Jesus, calling out with a loud voice, said, *"Father, into your hands I commit my spirit!"* And having said this he breathed his last.

Hebrews 5:7—In the days of his flesh, Jesus offered up prayers and supplications, with loud cries and tears, to him who was able to save him from death, and he was heard because of his reverence.

† † †

Jesus Prayed with Intercessions for Others

Mark 10:16—And he took [the children] in his arms and blessed them, laying his hands on them.

Luke 22:31-32—Simon, Simon, behold, Satan demanded to have you, that he might sift you like wheat, but I have prayed for you that your faith may not fail. And when you have turned again, strengthen your brothers.

John 14:16—And I will ask the Father, and he will give you another Helper, to be with you forever.

John 17:9, 20—*I am praying for them. I am not praying for the world but for those whom you have given me, for they are yours .... I do not ask for these only, but also for those who will believe in me through their word* .... (see the whole chapter)

Luke 23:46—And Jesus said, *"Father, forgive them, for they know not what they do."*

Luke 24:50-51—And he led them out as far as Bethany, and lifting up his hands he blessed them. While he blessed them, he parted from them and was carried up into heaven.

Fifty Commands to Pray in Scripture

† † †

Ten General Commands to Pray Always, in Every Place and for Everyone

1. Luke 18:1—[We] ought always to pray and not lose heart.

2. Luke 21:36—But stay awake at all times, praying that you may have strength .... (cf. 1 Pet. 4:7)

3. Romans 12:12—Be constant in prayer.

4. Ephesians 6:18a—Praying at all times in the Spirit, with all prayer and supplication.

5. Ephesians 6:18b—To that end, keep alert with all perseverance, making supplication for all the saints.

6. Philippians 4:6—But in everything by prayer and supplication with thanksgiving let your requests be made known to God.

7. Colossians 4:2—Continue steadfastly in prayer, being watchful in it with thanksgiving.

8. 1 Thessalonians 5:17-18 —Pray without ceasing, give thanks in all circumstances; for this is the will of God in Christ Jesus for you.

9. 1 Timothy 2:1—I urge that supplications, prayers, intercessions, and thanksgivings be made for all people.

10. 1 Timothy 2:8—I desire then that in every place the men should pray, lifting holy hands.

† † †

Ten Commands to Pray with Thanksgiving and Praise

1. Psalm 50:14-15—Offer to God a sacrifice of thanksgiving, and perform your vows to the Most High, and call upon me in the day of trouble; I will deliver you, and you shall glorify me. (cf. Psa. 116:17)

2. Psalm 105:1-4—Oh give thanks to the LORD; call upon his name; make known his deeds among the peoples! Sing to him, sing praises to him; tell of all his wondrous works! Glory in his holy name; let the hearts of those who seek the LORD rejoice! Seek the LORD and his strength; seek his presence continually! (cf. 1 Chronicles 16:8-11)

3. Ephesians 5:18, 20—Be filled with the Spirit, … giving thanks always and for everything to God the Father in the name of our Lord Jesus Christ.

4. Philippians 4:6—But in everything by prayer and supplication with thanksgiving let your requests be made known to God.

5. Colossians 2:6-7—Therefore, as you received Christ Jesus the Lord, so walk in him, … abounding in thanksgiving. (cf. Eph. 5:4)

6. Colossians 3:15, 17—And be thankful …. And whatever you

do, in word or deed, do everything in the name of the Lord Jesus, giving thanks to God the Father through him.

7. Colossians 4:2—Continue steadfastly in prayer, being watchful in it with thanksgiving.

8. 1 Thessalonians 5:17-18—Pray without ceasing, give thanks in all circumstances; for this is the will of God in Christ Jesus for you.

9. Hebrews 12:28-29—Therefore let us be grateful for receiving a kingdom that cannot be shaken, and thus let us offer to God acceptable worship, with reverence and awe, for our God is a consuming fire.

10. Hebrews 13:15—Through Jesus then let us continually offer up a sacrifice of praise to God, that is, the fruit of lips that acknowledge his name.

† † †

Ten Commands to Pray with Confession and Repentance

1. 2 Chronicles 7:13-14—When I [send affliction to] … my people, if my people who are called by my name humble themselves, and pray and seek my face and turn from their wicked ways, then I will hear from heaven and will forgive their sin and heal their land.

2. 2 Chronicles 30:6, 8-9—O people of Israel, return to the LORD …. Do not now be stiff-necked as your fathers were, but yield yourselves to the LORD and come to his sanctuary, which he has consecrated forever, and serve the LORD your God, that his fierce anger may turn away from you …. For the LORD

your God is gracious and merciful and will not turn away his face from you, if you return to him.

3. Isaiah 44:22—I have blotted out your transgressions like a cloud and your sins like mist; return to me, for I have redeemed you.

4. Isaiah 55:6-7—Seek the LORD while he may be found; call upon him while he is near; let the wicked forsake his way, and the unrighteous man his thoughts; let him return to the LORD, that he may have compassion on him, and to our God, for he will abundantly pardon.

5. Jeremiah 3:12-13, 22—Return, faithless Israel, declares the LORD. I will not look on you in anger, for I am merciful, declares the LORD; I will not be angry forever. Only acknowledge your guilt, that you rebelled against the LORD your God .... Return, O faithless sons; I will heal your faithlessness. "Behold, we come to you, for you are the LORD our God."

6. Hosea 12:6, 14:1-2—So you, by the help of your God, return .... Return, O Israel, to the LORD your God, for you have stumbled because of your iniquity. Take with you words and return to the LORD.

7. Malachi 3:7—Return to me, and I will return to you, says the LORD of hosts. (cf. Zech. 1:3-4)

8. Acts 8:22—Repent, therefore, of this wickedness of yours, and pray to the Lord that, if possible, the intent of your heart may be forgiven you. (cf. Acts 2:21, 38; 3:19-20)

9. Acts 17:30—The times of ignorance God overlooked, but now he commands all people everywhere to repent.

10. 1 John 1:9—If we confess our sins, he is faithful and just to forgive us our sins and to cleanse us from all unrighteousness. (cf. Prov. 28:13)

† † †

Ten Commands to Pray with Supplication in Time of Need

1. Psalm 32:6—Therefore let everyone who is godly offer prayer to you at a time when you may be found; surely in the rush of great waters, they shall not reach him.

2. Psalm 50:14-15—Call upon me in the day of trouble; I will deliver you, and you shall glorify me. (cf. Psa. 116:17)

3. Zechariah 10:1—Ask rain from the LORD in the season of the spring rain, from the LORD who makes the storm clouds, and he will give them showers of rain, to everyone the vegetation in the field. (cf. Ezek. 36:37)

4. Matthew 6:6, 9—But when you pray, go into your room and shut the door and pray to your Father who is in secret. And your Father who sees in secret will reward you …. Pray then like this, "Our Father in heaven … Give us this day our daily bread, and forgive us our debts, as we also have forgiven our debtors. And lead us not into temptation but deliver us from [the evil one]." (cf. Luke 11:2-4)

5. Matthew 7:7—Ask, and it will be given to you; seek, and you will find; knock, and it will be opened to you. For everyone who asks receives, and the one who seeks finds, and to the one who knocks it will be opened.

6. Matthew 26:41—Watch and pray that you may not enter into temptation.

7. John 15:7, 16:24—If you abide in me, and my words abide in you, ask whatever you wish, and it will be done for you …. Until now you have asked nothing in my name. Ask, and you will receive, that your joy may be full.

8. Hebrews 4:16—Let us then with confidence draw near to the throne of grace, that we may receive mercy and find grace to help in time of need. (cf. Phil. 4:6-7)

9. James 1:5-6—If any of you lacks wisdom, let him ask God, who gives generously to all without reproach, and it will be given him. But let him ask in faith.

10. James 5:13—Is anyone among you suffering? Let him pray.

† † †

Ten Commands to Pray with Intercession for Others

1. Jeremiah 29:7—Seek the welfare of the city where I have sent you into exile, and pray to the LORD on its behalf, for in its welfare you will find your welfare. (cf. Psa. 122:6)

2. Matthew 5:44—But I say to you, love your enemies and pray for those who persecute you. (cf. Luke 6:28)

3. Matthew 9:37-38—The harvest is plentiful, but the laborers are few; therefore pray earnestly to the Lord of the harvest to send out laborers into his harvest. (cf. Luke 10:2)

4. Ephesians 6:18-20—To that end, keep alert with all perseverance, making supplication for all the saints, and also for me, that words may be given to me in opening my mouth boldly to proclaim the mystery of the gospel, for which I am an ambassador in chains, that I may declare it boldly, as I ought to speak.

5. Romans 15:30-32—I appeal to you, brothers, by our Lord Jesus Christ and by the love of the Spirit, to strive together with me in your prayers to God on my behalf, that I may be delivered from the unbelievers in Judea, and that my service for

Jerusalem may be acceptable to the saints, so that by God's will I may come to you with joy and be refreshed in your company.

6. 2 Corinthians 1:11 — You also must help us by prayer, so that many will give thanks on our behalf for the blessing granted us through the prayers of many.

7. Colossians 4:3-4 — At the same time, pray also for us, that God may open to us a door for the word, to declare the mystery of Christ, on account of which I am in prison — that I may make it clear, which is how I ought to speak.

8. 2 Thessalonians 3:1-2 — Finally, brothers, pray for us, that the word of the Lord may speed ahead and be honored, as happened among you, and that we may be delivered from wicked and evil men. For not all have faith. (cf. 1 Thess. 5:25; Heb. 13:18-19)

9. 1 Timothy 2:1-4 — First of all, then, I urge that supplications, prayers, intercessions, and thanksgivings be made for all people, for kings and all who are in high positions, that we may lead a peaceful and quiet life, godly and dignified in every way. This is good, and it is pleasing in the sight of God our Savior, who desires all people to be saved and to come to the knowledge of the truth.

10. James 5:16 — Therefore, confess your sins to one another and pray for one another, that you may be healed. The prayer of a righteous person has great power as it is working. (cf. Phil. 4:6-7)

Twenty Benedictions in Scripture

✝ ✝ ✝

Benedictions for Peace, Hope and Love

1. Numbers 6:23-27—Thus you shall bless the people of Israel: you shall say to them, "The LORD bless you and keep you; the LORD make his face to shine upon you and be gracious to you; the LORD lift up his countenance upon you and give you peace." So shall they put my name upon the people of Israel, and I will bless them.

2. Romans 15:5-6, 13, 33—May the God of endurance and encouragement grant you to live in such harmony with one another, in accord with Christ Jesus, that together you may with one voice glorify the God and Father of our Lord Jesus Christ …. May the God of hope fill you with all joy and peace in believing, so that by the power of the Holy Spirit you may abound in hope …. May the God of peace be with you all. Amen.

3. 2 Thessalonians 3:16, 18—Now may the Lord of peace himself give you peace at all times in every way. The Lord be with you all …. The grace of our Lord Jesus Christ be with you all.

4. Ephesians 6:23-24—Peace be to the brothers, and love with

faith, from God the Father and the Lord Jesus Christ. Grace be with all who love our Lord Jesus Christ with love incorruptible.

✝ ✝ ✝

Benedictions for Divine Enablement and for the Glory of God

5. 2 Thessalonians 2:16-17—Now may our Lord Jesus Christ himself, and God our Father, who loved us and gave us eternal comfort and good hope through grace, comfort your hearts and establish them in every good work and word.

6. Galatians 6:18—The grace of our Lord Jesus Christ be with your spirit, brothers. Amen. (cf. 1 Cor. 16:23-24; 2 Tim. 4:22)

7. 2 Corinthians 13:14—The grace of the Lord Jesus Christ and the love of God and the fellowship of the Holy Spirit be with you all.

8. 2 Peter 3:18—But grow in the grace and knowledge of our Lord and Savior Jesus Christ. To him be the glory both now and to the day of eternity. Amen.

9. Hebrews 13:20-21—Now may the God of peace who brought again from the dead our Lord Jesus, the great shepherd of the sheep, by the blood of the eternal covenant, equip you with everything good that you may do his will, working in us that which is pleasing in his sight, through Jesus Christ, to whom be glory forever and ever. Amen.

10. Ephesians 3:20-21—Now to him who is able to do far more abundantly than all that we ask or think, according to the power at work within us, to him be glory in the church and in Christ Jesus throughout all generations, forever and ever. Amen.

11. Philippians 4:20—To our God and Father be glory forever and ever. Amen.

12. 1 Peter 4:11—In order that in everything God may be glorified through Jesus Christ. To him belong glory and dominion forever and ever. Amen.

13. 1 Timothy 1:17—To the King of the ages, immortal, invisible, the only God, be honor and glory forever and ever. Amen.

14. 1 Timothy 6:15-16—He who is the blessed and only Sovereign, the King of kings and Lord of lords, who alone has immortality, who dwells in unapproachable light, whom no one has ever seen or can see. To him be honor and eternal dominion. Amen.

† † †

Benedictions on Christ's Second Coming and Our Final Salvation

15. 1 Thessalonians 3:11-13—Now may our God and Father himself, and our Lord Jesus, direct our way to you, and may the Lord make you increase and abound in love for one another and for all, as we do for you, so that he may establish your hearts blameless in holiness before our God and Father, at the coming of our Lord Jesus with all his saints.

16. 1 Thessalonians 5:23-24, 28—Now may the God of peace himself sanctify you completely, and may your whole spirit and soul and body be kept blameless at the coming of our Lord Jesus Christ. He who calls you is faithful; he will surely do it .... The grace of our Lord Jesus Christ be with you.

17. 1 Peter 5:10-11—And after you have suffered a little while, the God of all grace, who has called you to his eternal glory in Christ, will himself restore, confirm, strengthen, and establish you. To him be the dominion forever and ever. Amen.

18. Jude 24-25—Now to him who is able to keep you from stumbling and to present you blameless before the presence of his glory with great joy, to the only God, our Savior, through Jesus Christ our Lord, be glory, majesty, dominion, and authority, before all time and now and forever. Amen.

19. Revelation 1:4-6—Grace to you and peace from him who is and who was and who is to come, and from the seven spirits who are before his throne, and from Jesus Christ the faithful witness, the firstborn of the dead, and the ruler of kings on earth. To him who loves us and has freed us from our sins by his blood and made us a kingdom, priests to his God and Father, to him be glory and dominion forever and ever. Amen.

20. Revelation 22:20-21—He who testifies to these things says, "Surely I am coming soon." Amen. Come, Lord Jesus! The grace of the Lord Jesus be with all. Amen.

Appendix IV

Helpful Works on Prayer

From the works on prayer referenced in this book the following are recommended by the editor as the most helpful. Most of these are available in print or as ebooks, and almost all are currently accessible online at Internet Archive (archive.org).

† † †

Helpful Works from the 17th Century

1. *The Privy Key to Heaven* by Thomas Brooks, 1665 (228 pp.)[1]

    This is rightly considered the classic Puritan work on private prayer. Spurgeon said of Brooks, "He has dust of gold; for even in the margins of his books there are sentences of exceeding preciousness .... If you have never read his works, I almost envy you the joy of entering for the first time upon [them]."

2. *Closet Prayer: A Christian Duty* by Oliver Heywood, 1671 (120 pp.)[2]

    Though not as widely known as Brooks' classic work, this book is also exceptionally helpful for private prayer, and notably shorter.

3. *Praying Always* by William Gurnall, 1662 (251 pp.)[3]

    Praying Always is one section (the 11th) in Gurnall's *magnum opus* on spiritual warfare entitled *The Christian in Complete*

Armour. John Newton recommended Gurnall's work as the most helpful book for the Christian after the Bible. Spurgeon called it "peerless and priceless," testifying of how the Lord often used it to rekindle his "low-burning coals."

† † †
Helpful Works from the 19th Century

1. *A Treatise on Prayer* by Edward Bickersteth, 1819 (212 pp.) [4]

Bickersteth writes with exceptional clarity and straightforward simplicity in this well-rounded overview of prayer. His work is rich in practical advice and biblical counsel on common struggles related to prayer.

2. *Sermons on Prayer* by C.H. Spurgeon, 1854-1891 [5]

Prayer was a major theme of Spurgeon's life and teaching with over 125 of his sermons relating directly to the subject. The sermons noted are among his best on prayer.

3. *Writings on Prayer* by Octavius Winslow, 1841-1866 [6]

Winslow's writings are filled with theological insights, thrilling exaltations of Christ, and warm pastoral encouragements. His most helpful writings on prayer are found in, *The Lord's Prayer* (particularly chapters 1, 2, 8, 9), *Personal Declension and Revival of Religion in the Soul* (chapter 4), and *The Precious Things of God* (chapter 10).

4. *A Call to Prayer* by J.C. Ryle, 1867 (32 pp.) [7]

Ryle's concise work is rich with stirring exhortations to pray.

5. *The Hidden Life of Prayer* by David McIntyre, 1891 (98 pp.) [8]

McIntyre supplements his own writing with extensive sections of choice quotations on prayer from the past. Many have testified of how God has used this little chest of jewels to deepen their life of prayer.

6. *Family Prayers* by Edward Bickersteth, 1843 (412 pp.)[9] and *Family Prayers* by Henry Law, 1868 (367 pp.)[10]

From among various collections of older prayers, these two works stand out as among the most edifying to read, ponder, and pray after. Other helpful collections of older prayers include:

- *Prayers and Offices of Devotions for Families* by Benjamin Jenks (1709)

- *Prayers for the Use of Families* by William Jay (1834)

- *The Practice of Piety* by Lewis Bayly (1842)

- *The Valley of Vision* by Arthur Bennett (1975)

- *Piercing Heaven* by Robert Elmer (2019)

✝ ✝ ✝

Helpful Works from the Early 20th Century

1. *The Prayer Life* by Andrew Murray, 1913 (114 pp.)[11]

Murray devoted much of his life and teaching to helping Christians pray. His best works on prayer include, *Lord, Teach Us to Pray* (1896), *The Ministry of Intercession* (1897), and *The Prayer Life* (1913). This final work of his is especially helpful to those desiring to overcome prayerlessness.

2. *The Kneeling Christian* by Albert Richardson, c. 1912-1930 (105 pp.)[12]

While serving as a missionary in Africa and India, Richardson learned the vital importance of prayer and later wrote this little book filled with illustrations of the power of prayer. He published it anonymously under the pseudonym, "The Unknown Christian."

3. *The Path of Prayer* by Samuel Chadwick, 1931 (128 pp.) [13]

After fifty years of a life devoted to prayer and preaching, Chadwick's devotional articles on prayer were eventually compiled and published into this work. *The Path of Prayer* is filled with practical wisdom and stirring exhortations.

† † †

Additional Helpful Works on Prayer

- *The Spirit of Prayer* by Nathaniel Vincent (1674)

- *A Guide to Prayer* by Isaac Watts (1715)

- *A Method for Prayer* by Matthew Henry (1712)

- *The Life of Prayer* by A.B. Simpson (1890)

- *Lessons in the School of Prayer* by A.T. Pierson (1895)

- *How to Pray* by R.A. Torrey (1900)

- *Prayer* by O. Hallesby (1931)

What a volume might be composed on the subject of prayer, and yet the half would not be told! A compilation of its achievements would of itself be the work of the longest life. Blessed are they who can enter into the spirit of these words, "I give myself unto prayer." [14]

~*Octavius Winslow (1808-1878)*

Sources

Most of the old English spellings and pronouns throughout this work have been modernized. Also, for comprehension, some archaic words have been substituted for contemporary ones and are noted by their placement in brackets. Words or phrases added for clarification or flow of thought are also placed in brackets, and any substantial deletions are noted with ellipses.

Part I: Taking Steps Forward in Prayer

1. John Flavel (c.1627-1691), "Sermon 24: The Second and Third Preparative for the Death of Christ" in *The Fountain of Life Opened Up*, 1671.

2. Anonymous

3. Octavius Winslow (1808-1878), "Going Home" in *Divine Realities: Spiritual Reflections for the Saint and Sinner*, 1860.

4. Thomas Manton (1620-1677), "Sermon No. 58 on Psalm 119:52" in *The Complete Works of Thomas Manton*, vol. 7 (London: Nisbet, 1873).

One: Initial Steps toward Prayer

1. E.M. Bounds (1835-1913), *The Necessity of Prayer* (New York: Fleming H. Revell Co, 1929).

2. James Hastings (1852-1922), *The Christian Doctrine of Prayer* (New York: Scribner's Sons, 1915) 419.

3. John MacDuff (1818-1895), *Grapes of Eschol*, 1861.

4. George Swinnock (1627-1673), "The Christian Man's Calling" in *The Works of George Swinnock*, vol.1 (Edinburgh: Nichol, 1868). First pub. 1662.

5. Thomas Manton (1620-1677), "Sermon No. 40 on Psalm 119:36" in *The Complete Works of Thomas Manton*, vol. 7 (London: Nisbet, 1873).

6. Thomas Manton (1620-1677), "Sermon No. 3 on Psalm 119:2" in *The Complete Works of Thomas Manton*, vol. 6 (London: Nisbet, 1872).

7. Thomas Manton (1620-1677), "Sermon No. 6 on 2nd Thessalonians 3:5" in *The Complete Works of Thomas Manton*, vol. 2 (London: Nisbet, 1871).

8. Thomas Manton (1620-1677), "Sermon No. 21 on Psalm 119:20" in *The Complete Works of Thomas Manton*, vol. 7 (London: Nisbet, 1873).

9. Isaac Ambrose (1604-1664), *Looking unto Jesus*, 1658.

10. A.W. Tozer (1897-1963), *The Pursuit of God*, (Abbotsford, WI: Aneko Press, 2015). First pub. 1948.

11. Ibid.

12. George Swinnock (1627-1673), "The Christian Man's Calling" in *The Works of George Swinnock*, vol.1 (Edinburgh: Nichol, 1868). First pub. 1662.

13. Edward Bickersteth (1786-1850), *A Treatise on Prayer* (Schenectady, NY: A. Van Santvoord & M. Cole, 1822). First pub. 1819.

14. C.H. Spurgeon (1834-1892), Lions Lacking But the Children Satisfied, Sermon No. 65 on Psa. 34:10, 1856.

15. Bernard of Clairvaux (c. 1090-1153), "Jesus, Thou Joy of Loving Hearts" in *The Sabbath Hymn and Tune Book* (New York: Masson Bros., 1859). Trans. by Ray Palmer.

16. A.W. Tozer (1897-1963), *The Pursuit of God*, (Abbotsford, WI: Aneko Press, 2015). First pub. 1948.

17. Isaac Ambrose (1604-1664), *Looking unto Jesus*, 1658.

18. Benjamin Jenks (1646-1724), *Prayers and Offices of Devotion*, (London: Longman & Co., 1837).

19. Ibid.

20. Isaac Ambrose (1604-1664), *Looking unto Jesus*, 1658.

21. Thomas Brooks (1608-1680), *The Privy Key of Heaven*, 1665.

22. R.A. Torrey (1856-1928), "Walking as Jesus Walked" in *The Voice of God in the Present Hour*, 1917.

23. J. Oswald Sanders (1902-1992), *The Incomparable Christ* (Chicago: Moody Publishers, 1971), 193.

24. Henry Scougal (1650-1678), *The Life of God in the Soul of Man*, 1677.

25. J.C. Ryle (1816-1900), *A Call to Prayer*, 1867.

26. Oliver Heywood (1630-1702), "Closet Prayer: A Christian Duty" in *The Whole Works of* ..., vol. 3 (Idle: Vint, 1825). First pub. 1671.

27. Octavius Winslow (1808-1878), *Consider Jesus: Thoughts for Daily Duty, Service, and Suffering*, 1870.

28. Thomas Brooks (1608-1680), *The Privy Key of Heaven*, 1665.

29. James Montgomery (1771-1854), "Prayer Is the Soul's Sincere Desire" in *Christian Psalmist* (Glasgow: Chalmers & Collins, 1825).

30. Andrew Murray (1828-1917), *With Christ in the School of Prayer*, 1884.

31. Martyn Lloyd-Jones (1899-1981), *Praying In The Spirit*, Sermon No. 4250 on Ephesians 6:18.

32. Amy Carmichael (1867-1951), *Overweights of Joy*, 1906.

33. Samuel Chadwick (1860-1932), *The Path of Prayer* (Fort Washington, PA: CLC Publications, 2000), 23. First pub. 1931.

34. J.H. Jowett (1864-1923), *The Preacher, His Life and Work*, 1912.

35. Andrew Murray (1828-1917), *The Ministry of Intercession: A Plea for More Prayer*, 1898.

36. Andrew Murray (1828-1917), *The Ministry of Intercession: A Plea for More Prayer*, 1898.

37. G. Campbell Morgan (1863-1945), *The Practice of Prayer* (New York: Fleming H. Revell Co., 1906), 49.

38. Henry Law (1797-1884), *Family Prayers* (London: Nisbet, 1868).

39. George Swinnock (1627-1673), "The Christian Man's Calling" in *The Works of George Swinnock*, vol.1 (Edinburgh: Nichol, 1868). First pub. 1662.

40. Jeremiah Burroughs (1599-1646), *The Rare Jewel of Christian Contentment*, 1648.

41. George Swinnock (1627-1673), "The Christian Man's Calling" in *The Works of George Swinnock*, vol.1 (Edinburgh: Nichol, 1868). First pub. 1662.

42. Thomas Brooks (1608-1680), *The Privy Key of Heaven*, 1665.

43. O. Hallesby (1879-1961), *Prayer* (Minneapolis: Augsburg Fortress, 1994), 15.

44. Thomas Manton (1620-1677), "An Exposition with Notes on the Epistle of James" in *The Complete Works of Thomas Manton*, vol. 4 (London: Nisbet, 1871), First pub. 1693.

45. Andrew Murray (1828-1917), *Abide in Christ*, 1882.

46. Richard Sibbes (1577-1635), "The Witness of Salvation," a sermon on Rom. 8:15-16 in *The Complete Works of Richard Sibbes*, vol. 7 (Edinburgh: James Nichol, 1864).

47. John Preston (1587-1628), *The Golden Scepter* (London: R.B., 1638).

48. C.H. Spurgeon (1834-1892), *A Paradox*, Sermon No. 2050 on 2 Cor. 12:10, 1888.

49. Ibid.

50. Joseph Scriven (1819-1886), "What a Friend We Have in Jesus" in *Social Hymns, Original and Selected* edited by Horace Hastings, 1865. First penned 1855.

51. William Jay (1769-1853), *Prayers for the Use of Families* (New York: Dodd & Mead, 1834).

52. J.C. Ryle (1816-1900), *A Call to Prayer*, 1867.

53. Andrew Bonar (1810-1892), *Andrew A. Bonnar D.D. Diary and Letters.* Edited by Marjory Bonar (London: Hodder and Stoughton, 1894).

54. David Brainerd (1718-1747), *The Life and Diary of David Brainerd* by Jonathan Edwards (Lafayette IN: Sovereign Grace Publishers, 2001). First pub. 1749.

55. Andrew Bonar (1810-1892), *Andrew A. Bonnar D.D. Diary and Letters.* Edited by Marjory Bonar (London: Hodder and Stoughton, 1894).

56. Ibid.

57. J.C. Ryle (1816-1900), *A Call to Prayer*, 1867.

58. John Flavel (c.1627-1691), *The Method of Grace in the Gospel of Redemption*, 1680.

59. Alexander Whyte (1836-1921), *Lord, Teach Us to Pray*, 1922.

60. J.C. Ryle (1816-1900), *A Call to Prayer*, 1867.

61. Octavius Winslow (1808-1878), *Personal Declension & Revival of Religion in the Soul* (New York: Robert Cater, 1847).

62. Oliver Heywood (1630-1702), *Closet Prayer: A Christian Duty*, 1671.

63. William Cowper (1731-1800), "O for a Closer Walk with God" in Collection of Psalms & Hymns, 1772.

64. Henry Law (1797-1884), *Family Prayers* (London: Nisbet, 1868).

65. John Owen (1616-1683), *Treatise of the Dominion of Sin and Grace*, 1688.

66. Gordon Watt (1865-1928), *Effectual Fervent Prayer* (Los Angeles: Biola Book Room, 1927)

67. George Swinnock (1627-1673), "The Christian Man's Calling" in *The Works of George Swinnock,* vol.1 (Edinburgh: Nichol, 1868). First pub. 1662.

68. C.H. Spurgeon (1834-1892), *Hindrances to Prayer*, Sermon No. 1192 on 1 Pet. 3:7, 1874.

69. R.A. Torrey (1856-1928), *How to Pray*, 1900.

70. William Cowper (1731-1800), "O for a Closer Walk with God" in Collection of Psalms & Hymns, 1772.

71. A.B. Simpson (1843-1919), *The Life of Prayer*, 1890.

72. John "Praying" Hyde (1865-1912), *The Life and Letters of Praying Hyde* by Gracia Hyde Bone, Mary Hyde Hall, ed. by Jerry Soen (CreateSpace, 2014), 59.

73. A.B. Simpson (1843-1919), *The Life of Prayer*, 1890.

74. Henry Law (1797-1884), *Family Prayers* (London: Nisbet, 1868).

75. Ibid.

76. A.B. Simpson (1843-1919), *The Life of Prayer*, 1890.

77. Ibid.

78. Octavius Winslow (1808-1878), *The Lord's Prayer: Its Spirit and Its Teaching*, 1866.

79. Ibid.

80. William Jay (1769-1853), *Prayers for the Use of Families* (New York: Dodd & Mead, 1834).

81. Thomas Manton (1620-1677), "Sermons Upon the Eighth Chapter of Romans: Sermon No. 7 on Rom. 8:5" in *The Complete Works of Thomas Manton*, vol. 12 (London: Nisbet, 1873).

82. Andrew Murray (1828-1917), *The Prayer Life* (Abbotsford, WI: Aneko Press, 2018) 103. First pub. 1913.

83. Thomas Boston (1676-1732), "The Christian Warfare" in *The Complete Works of…*, vol. 6. (London: Tegg, 1853).

84. Octavius Winslow (1808-1878), *Personal Declension & Revival of Religion in the Soul* (New York: Robert Cater, 1847).

85. Henry Law (1797-1884), *Family Prayers* (London: Nisbet, 1868).

86. Richard Baxter (1615-1691) *A Christian Directory*, vol. 1, 1673.

87. C.H. Spurgeon (1834-1892) *The Golden Key of Prayer*, Sermon No. 619 on Jer. 33:3, 1865.

88. C.H. Spurgeon (1834-1892), *Hindrances to Prayer*, Sermon No. 1192 on 1 Pet. 3:7, 1874.

89. Octavius Winslow (1808-1878), *Personal Declension & Revival of Religion in the Soul* (New York: Robert Cater, 1847).

90. William Gurnall (1616-1679), "Praying Always" in *The Christian in Complete Armour*. 1662-1665.

91. Richard Baxter (1615-1691), *A Christian Directory*, vol. 1, 1673.

92. J.C. Ryle (1816-1900), *A Call to Prayer*, 1867.

93. Andrew Murray (1828-1917) *The Ministry of Intercession: A Plea for More Prayer*, 1898.

94. Octavius Winslow (1808-1878), "The Cross of Christ the Christian's Weapon" in *The Foot of the Cross*, 1864.

95. Robert Leighton (1611-1684), *A Practical Commentary upon the First Epistle General of Peter*, c.1693.

96. William Gurnall (1616-1679) "Praying Always" in *The Christian in Complete Armour*, 1662-1665.

97. Edward Bickersteth (1786-1850), *Family Prayers* (Philadelphia: H. Hooker, 1843).

98. Philip Doddridge (1702-1751), *The Rise and Progress of Religion in the Soul*, 1745.

Two: Practical Steps toward Prayer

1. S.D. Gordon (1859-1936), *Quiet Talks on Prayer*, (New York: Fleming H. Revell Co., 1904), 12.

2. S.D. Gordon (1859-1936), *Quiet Talks on Prayer*, (New York: Fleming H. Revell Co., 1904), 16-17.

3. J. Oswald Sanders (1902-1992), "Effective Prayer" in *World Prayer* (Littleton, CO: OMF International, 1999), 14.

4. Thomas Brooks (1608-1680), *The Privy Key of Heaven*, 1665.

5. C.H. Spurgeon (1834-1892), *Hindrances to Prayer*, Sermon No. 1192 on 1 Pet. 3:7, 1874.

6. Ibid.

7. Andrew Murray (1828-1917), *The Master's Indwelling*, 1895.

8. William Wilberforce (1759-1833), quoted in *Power Through Prayer* by Edward M. Bounds (London: Marshall Brothers, 1912).

9. Thomas Brooks (1608-1680), *The Privy Key of Heaven*, 1665.

10. William M. Clow (1853-1930), "The Energy of Prayer," in *Classic Sermons on Prayer*, compiled by Warren W. Wiersbe (Grand Rapids: Kregel, 1987), 63.

11. William Gurnall (1616-1679), "Praying Always" in *The Christian in Complete Armour*. 1662-1665.

12. Andrew Bonar (1810-1892), *Andrew A. Bonnar D.D. Diary and Letters*. Edited by Marjory Bonar (London: Hodder and Stoughton, 1894).

13. Thomas Manton (1620-1677), "A Practical Exposition Upon the 53rd Chapter of Isaiah: The Eleventh Verse" in *The Complete Works of Thomas Manton*, vol. 2 (London: Nisbet, 1871).

14. Thomas Brooks (1608-1680), *The Privy Key of Heaven*, 1665.

15. George Croly (1780-1860), "Spirit of God, Descend Upon my Heart" in *Lyra Britannica*, 1867.

16. O. Hallesby (1879-1961), *Prayer* (Minneapolis: Augsburg Fortress, 1994), 83.

17. C.H. Spurgeon (1834-1892), *Order and Argument in Prayer*, Sermon No. 700 on Job 23:3-4, 1866.

18. Isaac Watts (1674-1748), *A Guide to Prayer*, 1715.

19. Oswald Chambers (1874-1917), *Christian Disciplines* (London: Marshall, Morgan & Scott, 1996).

20. J.O. Fraser (1886-1938), "The Prayer of Faith" in *Behind the Ranges* by Geraldine Taylor (Littleton, CO: OMF International, 1998), 124.

21. C.H. Spurgeon (1834-1892), *True Prayer True Power*, Sermon No. 328 on Mark 11:24, 1860.

22. Andrew Murray (1828-1917), *The Prayer Life* (Abbotsford, WI: Aneko Press, 2018) 79. First pub. 1913.

23. Frances R. Havergal (1836-1879), *Royal Commandments* (London: J. Nisbet & Co., 1877).

24. Samuel Lee (1625-1691), "The Morning Exercises" quoted in *The Treasury of David* (Psalm 142) by C.H. Spurgeon, 1885.

25. Matthew Henry (1662-1714), *A Method for* Prayer, 1712.

26. G. Campbell Morgan (1863-1945), *The Practice of Prayer* (New York: Fleming H. Revell Co., 1906), 111.

27. C.H. Spurgeon (1834-1892), *Praying in the Holy Spirit*, Sermon No. 719 on Jude 1:20, 1866.

28. Edward Bickersteth (1786-1850), *Family Prayers* (Philadelphia: H. Hooker, 1843).

29. J.C. Ryle (1816-1900), *Expository Thoughts on the* Gospels on Matt. 6:1-8, 1856.

30. A.T. Pierson (1837-1911), *Lessons in the School of Prayer* (New York: Anson D.F. Randolph & Co., 1895).

31. Thomas Brooks (1608-1680), *The Privy Key of Heaven*, 1665.

32. A.T. Pierson (1837-1911), *Lessons in the School of Prayer* (New York: Anson D.F. Randolph & Co., 1895).

33. Anonymous.

34. Richard Alleine (1610-1681), *Heaven Opened*, 1665.

35. C.H. Spurgeon (1834-1892), *Hindrances to Prayer*, Sermon No. 1192 on 1 Pet. 3:7, 1874.

36 J. Oswald Sanders (1902-1992), "Effective Prayer" in *World Prayer* (Littleton, CO: OMF International, 1999), 58-59.

37. Attributed to A.T. Pierson (1837-1911), Original source unknown.

38. J. Oswald Sanders (1902-1992), "Effective Prayer" in *World Prayer* (Littleton, CO: OMF International, 1999), 57.

39. William E. Sangster (1900-1960), "When I Find it Hard to Pray," in *Classic*

Sermons on Prayer, compiled by Warren W. Wiersbe (Grand Rapids: Kregel, 1987), 152.

40. J. Oswald Sanders (1902-1992), *Prayer Power Unlimited* (Grand Rapids: Discovery House Publishers, 1977), 134.

41. Samuel Chadwick (1860-1932), *The Path of Prayer* (Fort Washington, PA: CLC Publications,

2000), 29. First pub. 1931.

42. William E. Sangster (1900-1960), *Teach Me to Pray* (Nashville: The Upper Room, 1959), 11.

43. C.H. Spurgeon (1834-1892), *Daniel's Undaunted Courage*, Sermon on Dan. 6:10, 1868.

44. Matthew Henry (1662-1714), *Matthew Henry Commentary on the Whole Bible*, Daniel 6, First pub. 1708-1710

45. Thomas Manton (1620-1677), "A Practical Exposition of the Lord's Prayer" in *The Complete Works of Thomas Manton*, vol. 1 (London: Nisbet, 1870).

46. J. Oswald Sanders (1902-1992), "Effective Prayer" in *World Prayer* (Littleton, CO: OMF International, 1999), 59.

47. Edward Bickersteth (1786-1850), *Family Prayers* (Philadelphia: H. Hooker, 1843).

48. William Gurnall (1616-1679), "Praying Always" in *The Christian in Complete Armour*, 1662-1665.

49. David McIntyre (1859-1938), *The Hidden Life of Prayer*, 1891.

50. C.H. Spurgeon (1834-1892), *Let Us Pray*, Sermon No. 288 on Psa. 73:28, 1859.

51. Forbes Robinson (1867-1904), *Letters to His Friends* (New York: Longmans, Green & Co., 1909). First pub. 1904.

52. Amy Carmichael (1867-1951), *Whispers of His Power* (Old Tappan, NJ: Fleming H. Revell Company, 1982).

53. William E. Sangster (1900-1960), "When I Find it Hard to Pray," in *Classic Sermons on Prayer*, compiled by Warren W. Wiersbe (Grand Rapids: Kregel, 1987), 156.

54. Cotton Mather (1663-1728), *Diary of Cotton Mather* (Boston: Massachusetts Historical Society, 1911).

55. C.H. Spurgeon (1834-1892), *Comfort for Those Whose Prayers are Feeble*, Sermon No. 3083 Lam. 3:56, pub. 1908.

56. Ibid.

57. C.H. Spurgeon (1834-1892), *A Call to Prayer and Testimony*, Sermon No. 2189 on Isa. 62:6-7, 1891.

58. Jonathan Edwards (1703-1758), *Hypocrites Deficient in the Duty of Prayer*, Sermon on Job 27:10.

59. Andrew Bonar (1810-1892), *Andrew A. Bonnar D.D. Diary and Letters.* Edited by Marjory Bonar (London: Hodder and Stoughton, 1894).

60. Andrew Murray (1828-1917), *The Prayer Life* (Abbotsford, WI: Aneko Press, 2018) 133. First pub. 1913.

61. Edward Bickersteth (1786-1850), *Family Prayers* (Philadelphia: H. Hooker, 1843).

62. J.C. Ryle (1816-1900), *Expository Thoughts on the Gospels* on Mark 14:32-42, 1857.

63. William Gurnall (1616-1679), "Praying Always" in *The Christian in Complete Armour,* 1662-1665..

64. Richard Baxter (1615-1691), *A Christian Directory,* vol. 1, 1673.

65. William Gurnall (1616-1679), "Praying Always" in *The Christian in Complete Armour,* 1662-1665.

66. David Clarkson (1622-1686), "Pray for Everything," Sermon on Philippians 4:6 in *The Practical Works of David Clarkson,* vol. 2. First pub. 1697.

67. Oliver Heywood (1630-1702), *Closet Prayer: A Christian Duty,* 1671.

68. Thomas Manton (1620-1677), "An Exposition with Notes on the Epistle of James" in *The Complete Works of Thomas Manton,* vol. 4 (London: Nisbet, 1871). First pub. 1693.

69. Jonathan Edwards (1703-1758), "To Prepare Men's Hearts and Then to Answer Their Prayers," a sermon on Psalm 10:17 in *The Glory and Honor of God*, vol.2, by Michael McMullen (Nashville: Broadman & Holman, 2004) 100.

70. John Preston (1587-1628), *The Golden Scepter* (London: R.B., 1638).

71. Horatius Bonar (1808-1889), "Begin with God," *Hymns of Faith and Hope,* 1854.

72. Oliver Heywood (1630-1702), *Closet Prayer: A Christian Duty,* 1671.

73. Thomas Manton (1620-1677), "Sermon No. 117 on Psalm 119:107" in *The Complete Works of Thomas Manton,* vol. 7 (London: Nisbet, 1873).

74. Edward Bickersteth (1786-1850), *Family Prayers* (Philadelphia: H. Hooker, 1843).

75. Samuel Knight (1759–1827), *Forms of Prayer: For the Use of Christian Families* (Halifax: N. Whitley, 1827).

76. Samuel Lee (1625-1691), "How to Manage Secret Prayer" in *The Morning Exercises at Cripplegate,* vol.2, edited by James Nichols (London: Tegg, 1844). First pub. 1676 & edited by Samuel Annesley.

77. William Bates (1625-1699) "On Divine Meditation" in *The Whole Works of the Reverend William Bates*, vol 3 (London: Farmer, 1815).

78. William Gurnall (1616-1679), "Praying Always" in *The Christian in Complete Armour*, 1662-1665.

79. George Swinnock (1627-1673), "The Christian Man's Calling" in *The Works of George Swinnock*, vol.1 (Edinburgh: Nichol, 1868). First pub. 1662.

80. George Swinnock (1627-1673), "The Christian Man's Calling" in *The Works of George Swinnock*, vol.1 (Edinburgh: Nichol, 1868). First pub. 1662.

81. C.H. Spurgeon (1834-1892), *Prayer Perfumed with Praise*, Sermon No. 1469 on Phil 4:6, 1879.

82. Amy Carmichael (1867-1951), *Whispers of His Power* (Old Tappan, NJ: Fleming H. Revell Company, 1982), 80.

83. Ibid., 44.

84. George Müller (1805-1898), *A Narrative of Some of the Lord's Dealings with George Muller*, Part 3, 1865.

85. Samuel Knight (1759–1827), *Forms of Prayer: For the Use of Christian Families* (Halifax: N. Whitley, 1827).

86. Matthew Henry (1662-1714), *Matthew Henry Commentary on the Whole Bible*, Exodus 30, First pub. 1708-1710

87. C.H. Spurgeon (1834-1892), *Zealots*, Sermon No. 639 on Luke 6:15, 1865.

88. Richard Baxter (1615-1691), *A Christian Directory*, vol. 1, 1673.

89. F.B. Meyer (1847-1929), "Prayer and Intercession" in *The Epistle to the Philippians: A Devotional Commentary*, (London: The Religious Tract Society, 1912).

90. Leonard Ravenhill (1907-1994), *Revival Praying* (Minneapolis: Bethany Fellowship, 1962), 87.

91. Ibid., 101.

92. Edward Bickersteth (1786-1850), *Family Prayers* (Philadelphia: H. Hooker, 1843).

93. Andrew Murray (1828-1917), *Working for God*, 1901.

94. John Laidlow (1832-1906), quoted in *The Hidden Life of Prayer* by David McIntyre, 1891.

95. Albert Richardson (1868-19__), *The Kneeling Christian*, First pub. c. 1912-1930.

96. J.C. Ryle (1816-1900), *A Call to Prayer*, 1867.

97. A.B. Simpson (1843-1919), *The Life of Prayer*, 1890.

98. Oliver Heywood (1630-1702), *Closet Prayer: A Christian Duty*, 1671.

99. William Gurnall (1616-1679), "Praying Always" in *The Christian in Complete Armour*, 1662-1665.

100. Martin Luther (1483-1546), quoted by Thomas Brooks in *The Privy Key of Heaven*, 1665.

101. Thomas Brooks (1608-1680), *The Privy Key of Heaven*, 1665.

102. Andrew Murray (1828-1917), *The Ministry of Intercession: A Plea for More Prayer*, 1898.

103. F.B. Meyer (1847-1929), "Prayer and Intercession" in *The Epistle to the Philippians: A Devotional Commentary*, (London: The Religious Tract Society, 1912).

104. O. Hallesby (1879-1961), *Prayer* (Minneapolis: Augsburg Fortress, 1994), 42.

105. Anselm of Canterbury (c. 1033-1109), *A Prayer Treasury* (Oxford: Lion Publishing, 1998), 46.

Three: Steps during Prayer

1. Richard Baxter (1615-1691), *A Christian Directory*, vol. 1, 1673.

2. Thomas Ridgley (1667-1734), *A Body of Divinity*, 1731.

3. David Clarkson (1622-1686), "Pray for Everything," Sermon on Philippians 4:6 in *The Practical Works of David Clarkson*, vol. 2, First pub. 1697.

4. William Gurnall (1616-1679), "Praying Always" in *The Christian in Complete Armour*. 1662-1665.

5. Robert Leighton (1611-1684), "An Exposition of the Lord's Prayer," in *The Genuine Works of Robert Leighton*, vol. 3 (London: William Baynes & Son, 1822).

6. Unknown, attributed to Phillips Brooks (1835-1893).

7. Octavius Winslow (1808-1878), *The Holy Spirit, An Experimental and Practical View*, 1840.

8. Ibid.

9. Henry Law (1797-1884), *Family Prayers* (London: Nisbet, 1868).

10. Philip Doddridge (1702-1751), *The Rise and Progress of Religion in the Soul*, 1745.

11. Amy Carmichael (1867-1951), *Whispers of His Power* (Old Tappan, NJ: Fleming H. Revell Company, 1982), 93.

12. John Calvin (1509-1564), *Institutes of the Christian Religion*, Book 3, Ch. 20, Section 4, First pub. 1536.

13. Richard Baxter (1615-1691), *A Christian Directory*, vol. 1, 1673.

14. C.H. Spurgeon (1834-1892), *Order and Argument in Prayer*, Sermon No. 700 on Job 23:3-4, 1866.

15. C.H. Spurgeon (1834-1892), *Concerning Prayer*, Sermon No. 2053 on Psa. 86:6-7, 1888.

16. Andrew Murray (1828-1917), *Lord, Teach Us to Pray*, 1896.

17. Andrew Murray (1828-1917), *God's Word for Growing in Prayer* (Uhrichsville, Ohio : Humble Creek, 2003), 12.

18. Samuel Chadwick (1860-1932), *The Path of Prayer* (Fort Washington, PA: CLC Publications, 2000) 36. First pub. 1931.

19. Anthony Burgess (1600-1663), "Sermon No. 24: Of Vain Tautology in Prayer" on John 17:5 in *Christ's Prayer Before His Passion: Expository Sermons on John 17* (London: Abraham Miller, 1656).

20. Robert Leighton (1611-1684), "An Exposition of the Lord's Prayer," in *The Genuine Works of Robert Leighton*, vol. 3 (London: William Baynes & Son, 1822).

21. Samuel Chadwick (1860-1932), *The Path of Prayer* (Fort Washington, PA: CLC Publications, 2000), 36. First pub. 1931.

22. Andrew Murray (1828-1917), *The Inner Chamber and The Inner Life*, 1905.

23. Octavius Winslow (1808-1878), *Consider Jesus: Thoughts for Daily Duty, Service, and Suffering*, 1870.

24. F.B. Meyer (1847-1929), quoted in *Thoughts for the Quiet Hour*, ed. by D.L. Moody, 1881.

25. Robert Leighton (1611-1684), "An Exposition of the Lord's Prayer," in *The Genuine Works of Robert Leighton*, vol. 3 (London: William Baynes & Son, 1822).

26. Henry Law (1797-1884), *Family Prayers* (London: Nisbet, 1868).

27. Susanna Wesley (1669-1742), *The Prayers of Susanna Wesley* by WL Douhgty (Grand Rapids: Zondervan, 1984), 26.

28. Edward Bickersteth (1786-1850), *A Treatise on Prayer* (Schenectady, NY: A. Van Santvoord & M. Cole, 1822). First pub. 1819.

29. Thomas Boston (1676-1732) "Saints Wrestling for the Blessing and Obtaining It" in *The Complete Works of ...*, vol. 3 (London: Tegg, 1853).

30. Thomas Boston (1676-1732) "The Believer's Hundredfold in this Life Considered" in *The Complete Works of ...*, vol. 5 (London: Tegg, 1853).

31. C.H. Spurgeon (1834-1892), *Wordless Prayers Heard in Heaven*, Sermon No. 2696 on Isa. 41:17, 1881.

32. Edward Bickersteth (1786-1850), *A Treatise on Prayer* (Schenectady, NY: A. Van Santvoord & M. Cole, 1822). First pub. 1819.

33. Thomas Boston (1676-1732) "The Nature of Prayer" in *The Complete Works of ...*, vol. 2 (London: Tegg, 1853).

34. F.B. Meyer (1847-1929), *Calvary to Pentecost* (New York: Leming H. Revell, 1894).

35. Edward Bickersteth (1786-1850), *A Treatise on Prayer* (Schenectady, NY: A. Van Santvoord & M. Cole, 1822). First pub. 1819.

36. George Swinnock (1627-1673), "Of the Concomitants of Prayer"" in *The Works of George Swinnock*, vol.1 (Edinburgh: Nichol, 1868). First pub. 1662.

37. Edward Bickersteth (1786-1850), *Family Prayers* (Philadelphia: H. Hooker, 1843).

38. Edward Bickersteth (1786-1850), *A Treatise on Prayer* (Schenectady, NY: A. Van Santvoord & M. Cole, 1822). First pub. 1819.

39. C.H. Spurgeon (1834-1892), *Pleading*, Sermon No. 1018 on Psa. 70:5, 1871.

40. C.H. Spurgeon (1834-1892), *Constant, Instant, Expectant*, Sermon No. 1480 on Rom. 12:12, 1879.

41. Edward Bickersteth (1786-1850), *A Treatise on Prayer* (Schenectady, NY: A. Van Santvoord & M. Cole, 1822). First pub. 1819.

42. Henry Law (1797-1884), *Family Prayers* (London: Nisbet, 1868).

43. Edward Bickersteth (1786-1850), *Family Prayers* (Philadelphia: H. Hooker, 1843).

44. William Gurnall (1616-1679), "Praying Always" in *The Christian in Complete Armour*. 1662-1665.

46. Horatius Bonar (1808-1889), *Light and Truth (IV) – Lesser Epistles*, 1870.

47. A.B. Simpson (1843-1919), *The Life of Prayer*, 1890.

48. John MacDuff (1818-1895), *Family Prayers*, 1885.

49. Samuel Knight (1759–1827), *Forms of Prayer: For the Use of Christian Families* (Halifax: N. Whitley, 1827).

50. Benjamin Jenks (1646-1724), *Prayers and Offices of Devotion*, (London: Longman & Co., 1837).

51. Lewis Bayly (c.1575-1631), *The Practice of Piety*, 1611.

52. Ibid.

53. Ibid.

54. C.H. Spurgeon (1834-1892), *Comfort for Those Whose Prayers are Feeble*, Sermon No. 3083 Lam. 3:56, pub. 1908.

55. R.A. Torrey (1856-1928), *How to Pray*, 1900.

56. William Gurnall (1616-1679), "Praying Always" in *The Christian in Complete Armour*. 1662-1665.

57. Ibid.

58. David McIntyre (1859-1938), *The Hidden Life of Prayer*, 1891.

59. C.H. Spurgeon (1834-1892), *Comfort for Those Whose Prayers are Feeble*, Sermon No. 3083 Lam. 3:56, pub. 1908.

60. David Clarkson (1622-1686), "Faith in Prayer," Sermon on James 1:6 in *The Practical Works of David Clarkson*, vol. 1, First pub. 1697.

61. George Müller (1805-1898), *A Narrative of Some of the Lord's Dealings with George Müller*, Part 1, 1865.

62. Edward Bickersteth (1786-1850), *Family Prayers* (Philadelphia: H. Hooker, 1843).

63. William Cowper (1731-1800), "Exhortation to Prayer," in *A Selection of Psalms and Hymns*, 1790.

64. Andrew Bonar (1810-1892), *Andrew A. Bonnar D.D. Diary and Letters*. Edited by Marjory Bonar (London: Hodder and Stoughton, 1894).

65. Martin Luther (1483-1546), *What Luther Says: An Anthology*, vol. 2, Ewald M. Plass, ed. (St. Louis: Concordia Publishing, 1959), 1083.

66. John Bunyan (1628-1688), quoted in *The Hidden Life of Prayer* by David McIntyre, 1891.

67. William Gurnall (1616-1679), "Praying Always" in *The Christian in Complete Armour*, 1662-1665.

68. Richard Baxter (1615-1691), *A Christian Directory*, vol. 1, 1673.

69. Albert Richardson (1868-19__), *The Kneeling Christian*, First pub. c. 1912-1930.

70. O. Hallesby (1879-1961), *Prayer* (Minneapolis: Augsburg Fortress, 1994), 115.

71. Oliver Heywood (1630-1702), *Closet Prayer: A Christian Duty*, 1671

72. David Clarkson (1622-1686), "Pray for Everything," Sermon on Philippians 4:6 in *The Practical Works of David Clarkson*, vol. 2. First pub. 1697.

73. William Gurnall (1616-1679), "Praying Always" in *The Christian in Complete Armour*. 1662-1665.

74. Richard Baxter (1615-1691), *A Christian Directory*, vol. 1, 1673.

75. C.H. Spurgeon (1834-1892), *C.H. Spurgeon's Prayers* (Grand Rapids: Baker, 1978), 25.

76. Thomas Manton (1620-1677), "How May We Cure Distractions in Holy Duties?" in *The Complete Works of Thomas Manton*, vol. 5 (London: Nisbet, 1873).

77. Thomas Manton (1620-1677), "Twenty Sermons on Important Passages of Scripture: Sermon No. 6 on 2 Thess. 3:5" in *The Complete Works of Thomas Manton*, vol. 2 (London: Nisbet, 1871)

78. William E. Sangster (1900-1960), "When I Find it Hard to Pray," in *Classic Sermons on Prayer*, compiled by Warren W. Wiersbe (Grand Rapids: Kregel, 1987), 155-156.

79. Edward Bickersteth (1786-1850), *A Treatise on Prayer* (Schenectady, NY: A. Van Santvoord & M. Cole, 1822). First pub. 1819.

80. Fredrick W. Faber (1814-1863), quoted in *The Christian Book of Mystic Verse*, ed. by A.W. Tozer, (Chicago, Moody Publishers, 1963) 99-100.

81. Edward Bickersteth (1786-1850), *Family Prayers* (Philadelphia: H. Hooker, 1843).

Four: Steps after Prayer

1. William Gurnall (1616-1679), "Praying Always" in *The Christian in Complete Armour*. 1662-1665.

2. Oliver Heywood (1630-1702), "Intercession of Christ" in *The Whole Works of …*, vol. 3 (Idle: Vint, 1825). First pub. 1701.

3. C.H. Spurgeon (1834-1892), *Golden Vials Full of Odors*, Sermon No. 1051 on Rev. 5:8, 1872.

4. Jonathan Edwards (1703-1758), "The Most High, A Prayer-Hearing God," A sermon on Psalm 62:5, in *The Works of Jonathan Edwards*, vol. 2 (Edinburgh: Banner of Truth, 1974).

5. C.H. Spurgeon (1834-1892), *Prayer Answered, Love Nourished*, Sermon No. 240 on Psa. 116:1, 1859.

6. J.C. Ryle (1816-1900), *Expository Thoughts on the* Gospels on Matt. 5:21-28, 1856.

7. Charles Wesley (1707-1788), "Jesus, My Strength, My Hope." Original title, "A Poor Sinner" in *Hymns & Sacred Poems*, 1742.

8. Henry Law (1797-1884), *Family Prayers* (London: Nisbet, 1868).

9. George Swinnock (1627-1673), "The Christian Man's Calling" in *The Works of George Swinnock*, vol.1 (Edinburgh: Nichol, 1868). First pub. 1662.

10. A.W. Tozer (1897-1963), *The Pursuit of God*, (Abbotsford, WI: Aneko Press, 2015), 99. First pub. 1948.

11. G. Campbell Morgan (1863-1945), *The Practice of Prayer* (New York: Fleming H. Revell Co., 1906), 113.

12. Alexander Maclaren (1826-1910), "Continual Prayer and It's Effects" on 1 Thess. 5:16-17 in *Expositions of Holy Scripture*, 1904-1910.

13. Alexander Maclaren (1826-1910), "Where and How to Pray" on 1 Tim. 2:8 in *Expositions of Holy Scripture*, 1904-1910.

14. James Hastings (1852-1922), *The Christian Doctrine of Prayer* (New York: Scribner's Sons, 1915) 419.

15. George Swinnock (1627-1673), "The Christian Man's Calling" in *The Works of George Swinnock*, vol.1 (Edinburgh: Nichol, 1868). First pub. 1662.

16. Ibid.

17. Andrew Bonar (1810-1892), *Andrew A. Bonnar D.D. Diary and Letters*. Edited by Marjory Bonar (London: Hodder and Stoughton, 1894).

18. Ibid.

19. Susanna Wesley (1669-1742), *Susanna Wesley Complete Writings* by Charles Wallace (New York: Oxford University Press, 1997). 228.

20. F.B. Meyer (1847-1929), "The Spirit's Help" in *The Present Tenses of the Blessed Life*, 1892.

21. Samuel Lee (1625-1691), "How to Manage Secret Prayer" in *The Morning Exercises at Cripplegate*, vol.2, edited by James Nichols (London: Tegg, 1844). First pub. 1676 & edited by Samuel Annesley.

22. Brother Lawrence (1614-1691), *The Practice of the Presence of God*, 1692.

23. C.H. Spurgeon (1834-1892), *Concerning Prayer*, Sermon No. 2053 on Psa. 86:6-7, 1888.

24. Robert Leighton (1611-1684), "An Exposition of the Lord's Prayer," in *The Genuine Works of Robert Leighton*, vol. 3 (London: William Baynes & Son, 1822).

25. William Jay (1769-1853), *Prayers for the Use of Families* (New York: Dodd & Mead, 1834).

26. Amy Carmichael (1867-1951), *Whispers of His Power* (Old Tappan, NJ: Fleming H. Revell Company, 1982), 102.

27. Andrew Murray (1828-1917), *The State of the Church*, 1912.

28. J.C. Ryle (1816-1900), *Practical Religion*, 1878.

29. J.C. Ryle (1816-1900), *A Call to Prayer*, 1867.

30. A.T. Pierson (1837-1911), *George Müller of Bristol*, 1899.

31. J.C. Ryle (1816-1900), *Expository Thoughts on the Gospels, Mark* (Mk. 7:24-30), 1857.

32. Ibid.

33. George Müller (1805-1898), *Autobiography of George Müller: Life of Trust*, 1861.

34. R.F. Horton (1855-1934), *My Belief* (New York: Fleming H. Revell Co., 1909).

35. Fanny Crosby (1820-1915), "The Lord Will Answer Prayer," in *Young People's Songs of Praise*, by I. Allan Sankey (Chicago: Bigelow & Main, 1902).

36. Jonathan Edwards (1703-1758), "The Most High, A Prayer-Hearing God," A sermon on Psalm 62:5, in *The Works of Jonathan Edwards*, vol. 2 (Edinburgh: Banner of Truth, 1974).

37. Nathaniel Vincent (c.1639-1697), *The Spirit of Prayer,* 1674.

38. William Gurnall (1616-1679), "Praying Always" in *The Christian in Complete Armour*, 1662-1665.

39. Henry Law (1797-1884), *Family Prayers* (London: Nisbet, 1868).

Part II: Approaching the Triune God

1. John Owen (1616-1683), "A Discourse of the Work of The Holy Spirit in Prayer" in *The Works of John Owen*, vol. 4, Edited by W. Goold (Edinburg: T & T Clark, 1862). First pub. 1682.

2. Andrew Murray (1828-1917), *The Prayer Life* (Abbotsford, WI: Aneko Press, 2018) 50. First pub. 1913.

3. Thomas Manton (1620-1677), "A Practical Commentary on the Epistle of Jude" in *The Complete Works of Thomas Manton*, vol. 5 (London: Nisbet, 1873).

4. A.B. Simpson (1843-1919), *Walking in the Spirit*, (New York: Christian Alliance Pub. Co., 1885)

5. G. Campbell Morgan (1863-1945), *The Practice of Prayer* (New York: Fleming H. Revell Co., 1906), 46.

6. Henry Law (1797-1884), *Family Prayers* (London: Nisbet, 1868).

Five: Praying to the Father

1. A.B. Simpson (1843-1919), *The Life of Prayer*, 1890

2. Martin Luther (1483-1546), "A Beautiful Easter Sermon" on Mark 16:1-8 in *Martin Luther Sermons*, vol. 2, edited by John Nicholas Lenker, 1905. First delivered 1538.

3. Martyn Lloyd-Jones (1899-1981), *Studies in the Sermon on the Mount*, (Grand Rapids: Eerdmans, 1971), 327.

4. Octavius Winslow (1808-1878), *The Lord's Prayer: Its Spirit and Its Teaching*, 1866.

5. Martyn Lloyd-Jones (1899-1981), *Studies in the Sermon on the Mount*, (Grand Rapids: Eerdmans, 1971), 308.

6. Edward Bickersteth (1786-1850), *Family Prayers* (Philadelphia: H. Hooker, 1843).

7. Stephen Charnock (1628-1680), "On the Goodness of God" in *Discourses Upon the Existence and Attributes of God* (London: Henry G. Bohn, 1853). First pub. posthumously 1682.

8. Alexander Maclaren (1826-1910), "How to Pray" on Luke 11:1-13 in *Expositions of Holy Scripture: St. Luke*, 1904-1910.

9. David Brainerd (1718-1747), *The Life and Diary of David Brainerd* by Jonathan Edwards (Lafayette IN: Sovereign Grace Publishers, 2001). First pub. 1749.

10. Benjamin Jenks (1646-1724), *Prayers and Offices of Devotion*, (London: Longman & Co., 1837).

11. John Owen (1616-1683), *Communion with God the Father, Son, and Holy Ghost*, edited by Kelley M. Kapic & Justin Taylor (Wheaton IL: Crossway, 2007). First pub. 1657.

12. J.C. Ryle (1816-1900), *Able to Save*, a sermon on Heb. 7:25.

13. Richard Baxter (1615-1691) *A Christian Directory*, vol. 1. First pub. 1673.

14. Thomas Boston (1676-1732) "The Preface of the Lord's Prayer" in *The Complete Works of ...*, vol. 2 (London: Tegg, 1853).

15. Benjamin Jenks (1646-1724), *Prayers and Offices of Devotion*, (London: Longman & Co., 1837).

16. C.H. Spurgeon (1834-1892), *The Pastor in Prayer* (Edinburgh: Banner of Truth, 2004). Sourced from *The Pastor in Prayer* (Elliot Stock: London, 1893).

17. William Gurnall (1616-1679) "Praying Always" in *The Christian in Complete Armour*. 1662-1665.

18. Octavius Winslow (1808-1878), *The Lord's Prayer: Its Spirit and Its Teaching*, 1866.

19. C.H. Spurgeon (1834-1892), *Heaven's Nurse Children*, Sermon No. 1021 on Hos. 11:3.

20. Thomas Brooks (1608-1680) *The Privy Key of Heaven*, 1665.

21. Andrew Murray (1828-1917) *With Christ in the School of Prayer*, 1884.

22. Henry Lyte (1793-1847), *Praise My Soul, the King of Heaven*, 1834.

23. Edward Bickersteth (1786-1850), *Family Prayers* (Philadelphia: H. Hooker, 1843).

24. A.B. Simpson (1843-1919), *Christ in the Bible: Epistles of John*, 1900.

25. A.B. Simpson (1843-1919), *Hard Places in the Way of Faith*, 1899.

26. Octavius Winslow (1808-1878), *The Lord's Prayer: Its Spirit and Its Teaching*, 1866.

27. Octavius Winslow (1808-1878), *The Glory of the Redeemer*, 1844.

28. Octavius Winslow (1808-1878), *Grace & Truth*, 1849.

29. A.B. Simpson (1843-1919), *Christ in the Bible: Epistles of John*, 1900.

30. Thomas Boston (1676-1732) "Discourses on Prayer" in *The Complete Works of …*, vol. 11 (London: Tegg, 1853).

31. Octavius Winslow (1808-1878), *Morning Thoughts*, Dec. 29 on 2 Sam. 22:29, 1856.

32. Horatius Bonar (1808-1889), "Ch. 83: Declaration of the Father's Name" in *Light and Truth (I): The Old Testament*, 1868.

33. Octavius Winslow (1808-1878), *Morning Thoughts*, Sept. 30 on Gal. 4:6, 1856.

34. A.B. Simpson (1843-1919), *Present Truth*, 1897.

35. Octavius Winslow (1808-1878), *The Lord's Prayer: Its Spirit and Its Teaching*, 1866.

36. R.A. Torrey (1856-1928), *The Person & Work of the Holy Spirit*, 1910.

37. Ibid.

38. Ibid.

39. Anthony Burgess (1600-1663), "Sermon No. 135: Of a Humbled Christian Improving in His Prayers …" on John 17:24 in *Christ's Prayer Before His Passion: Expository Sermons on John 17* (London: Abraham Miller, 1656).

40. Lewis Bayly (c.1575-1631), *The Practice of Piety*, 1611.

41. Martyn Lloyd-Jones (1899-1981), *Praying in the Spirit*, Sermon No. 4060 on Ephesians 2:18.

42. Andrew Murray (1828-1917) *The New Life: Words of God for Young Disciples of Christ*, 1891.

43. Andrew Murray (1828-1917) *The Prayer Life* (Abbotsford, WI: Aneko Press, 2018) 114. First pub. 1913.

44. Andrew Murray (1828-1917) *The Inner Chamber and The Inner Life*, 1905.

45. Thomas Manton (1620-1677), "Sermons Upon The Eighth Chapter of Romans: Sermon No. 35 on Rom. 8:26" in *The Complete Works of Thomas Manton,* vol. 12 (London: Nisbet, 1873).

46. John Bradford (1510-1555), "The Restoration of All Things" in *The Writ-*

ings of the Rev. John Bradford, edited by Aubrey Townsend (Cambridge: University Press, 1848).

47. John Owen (1616-1683), *Communion with God the Father, Son, and Holy Ghost*, edited by Kelley M. Kapic & Justin Taylor (Wheaton IL: Crossway, 2007). First pub. 1657.

48. Thomas Manton (1620-1677), "A Practical Exposition of the Lord's Prayer" in *The Complete Works of Thomas Manton*, vol. 1 (London: Nisbet, 1870).

49. John Chrysostom (347-407), *Homily 22* on Matthew 5:28-29.

50. Benjamin Jenks (1646-1724), *Prayers and Offices of Devotion*, (London: Longman & Co., 1837).

Six: Praying through the Son

1. Oliver Heywood (1630-1702), *Closet Prayer: A Christian Duty*, 1671.

2. Oliver Heywood (1630-1702), *Intercession of Christ*, 1701.

3. C.H. Spurgeon (1834-1892), *The Mediator – The Interpreter*, Sermon No. 2097 on Ex. 20:18-20, 1889.

4. Isaac Watts (1674-1748), *A Guide to Prayer*, 1715.

5. Thomas Boston (1676-1732), "The Nature of Prayer" in *The Complete Works of...*, vol. 2 (London: Tegg, 1853).

6. John MacDuff (1818-1895), *Memories of Gennesaret*, 1859.

7. Thomas Boston (1676-1732) "A Discourse on the Experimental Knowledge of Christ," in *The Complete Works of...*, vol. 2. (London: Tegg, 1853).

8. Philip Henry (1631-1696), *Christ is All in All*, pub. posthumously 1830.

9. Lewis Bayly (c.1575-1631), *The Practice of Piety*, 1611.

10. Matthew Henry (1662-1714), *Directions for Daily Communion with God*, 1712.

11. C.H. Spurgeon (1834-1892), *Behold, He Prays*, Sermon No. 1860 on Acts 9:11, 1885.

12. Ambrose of Milan (c. 340-397), quoted in *Treatise on Prayer* by John Knox (c.1514-1572).

13. C.H. Spurgeon (1834-1892), *Golden Vials Full of Odors*, Sermon No. 1051 on Rev. 5:8, 1872.

14. Thomas Brooks (1608-1680), *The Privy Key of Heaven*, 1665.

15. Lewis Bayly (c.1575-1631), *The Practice of Piety*, 1611.

16. Isaac Ambrose (1604-1664), *Looking Unto Jesus*, 1658.

17. Richard Baxter (1615-1691), *A Christian Directory*, vol. 2. First pub. 1673.

18. Richard Baxter (1615-1691), *A Christian Directory*, vol. 1. First pub. 1673.

19. Isaac Ambrose (1604-1664), *Looking Unto Jesus*, 1658.

20. Ibid.

21. Ibid.

22. R.A. Torrey (1856-1928), *How to Pray*, 1900.

23. Isaac Ambrose (1604-1664), *Looking Unto Jesus*, 1658.

24. Ibid.

25. Ibid.

26. Charles Wesley (1707-1788), "Arise, My Soul Arise," Original title "Behold the Man" in *Hymns & Sacred Poems*, 1742.

27. Edward Bickersteth (1786-1850), *Family Prayers* (Philadelphia: H. Hooker, 1843).

28. Octavius Winslow (1808-1878), "The Sympathy of the Spirit with the Infirmity of Prayer" in *No Condemnation in Christ Jesus*, 1852.

29. Octavius Winslow (1808-1878), "The Tried Believer Comforted" in *The Atonement*, 1839.

30. Isaac Ambrose (1604-1664), *Looking unto Jesus*, 1658.

31. Octavius Winslow (1808-1878), "Go and Tell Jesus" in *Divine Realities: Spiritual Reflections for the Saint and Sinner*, 1860.

32. Ibid.

33. Robert Murray M'Cheyne (1813-1843), *The Biography of Robert Murray M'Cheyne* by Andrew Bonar, 1844.

34. Horatius Bonar (1808-1889), "Tract 23: Salvation to the Uttermost" in *The Kelso Tracts*, 1846.

35. Octavius Winslow (1808-1878), "The Believers' Triumph" in *No Condemnation in Christ Jesus*, 1852.

36. Charite Lees (Smith) Bancroft (1841-1932), "Advocate," in *Our Own Hymnbook*, 1883. Penned in 1863.

37. Thomas Watson (1620-1686), "Christ's Priestly Office in "Part IV: The Covenant of Grace and Its Mediator" in *A Body of Practical Divinity*, 1686.

38. William Bridge (c. 1600-1670), Sermon No. 4 on Heb. 11:17-18 in "The Great Gospel Mystery … Christ's Priestly Office" in *The Works of William Bridge,* vol. 1 (London: E. Palmer & Son, 1845).

39. Octavius Winslow (1808-1878), "The Christian's Devout Acknowledgment of God" in *The Fullness of Christ*, 1863.

40. C.H. Spurgeon (1834-1892), *Blood Even on the Golden Altar*, Sermon No. 2369 on Lev. 4:7, 1888.

41. Octavius Winslow (1808-1878), *Personal Declension & Revival of Religion in the Soul* (New York: Robert Cater, 1847).

42. Andrew Murray (1828-1917), *The Holiest of All: An Exposition of The Epistle to the Hebrews*, 1894.

43. Robert Hawker (1753-1827), *The Poor Man's Morning and Evening Portions* (New York: Robert Wauchope, 1819).

44. Oliver Heywood (1630-1702), *Intercession of Christ*, 1701.

45. Cotton Mather (1663-1728), *Diary of Cotton Mather* (Boston: Massachusetts Historical Society, 1911).

46. Octavius Winslow (1808-1878), *Personal Declension & Revival of Religion in the Soul* (New York: Robert Cater, 1847).

47. C.H. Spurgeon (1834-1892), *The Sinners Advocate,* Sermon No. 515 on 1 John 2:1, 1863.

48. Alexander Maclaren (1826-1910), "The Throne of Grace" on Heb. 4:16 in *Expositions of the Holy Scripture: Hebrews*, 1904-1910.

49. Isaac Watts (1674-1748), "There is A Voice of Sovereign Grace," a cento from "How Sad Our State by Nature Is" in *Hymns & Sacred Songs*, 1707.

50. Anonymous, quoted in *A Stranger Here: Memorial to One to Whom to Live Was Christ, and to Die Was Gain*, by Horatius Bonar (1808-1889), 1852.

51. Charles Wesley (1707-1788), "Depth of Mercy! Can There Be" in *Hymns & Sacred Poems*, 1740.

52. Octavius Winslow (1808-1878), *The Holy Spirit, An Experimental and Practical View*, 1840.

53. Robert Murray M'Cheyne (1813-1843), *Memoir and Remains of the Rev. Robert Murray M'Cheyne*, 1844.

54. John Newton (1725-1807), "Approach My Soul, the Mercy Seat" in *Olney Hymns*. First pub. 1779.

55. Octavius Winslow (1808-1878), *Words of Divine Comfort*, 1872.

56. Henry Law (1797-1884), *Family Prayers* (London: Nisbet, 1868).

Seven: Praying in the Spirit

1. C.H. Spurgeon (1834-1892), *Our Urgent Need of the Holy Spirit*, Sermon No. 1332 on Rom. 15:13; 19, 1877.

2. Isaac Watts (1674-1748), *A Guide to Prayer*, 1715.

3. R. C. Trench (1807-1886), "Sermon No. 20: The Holy Trinity in Relation to Our Prayers" on Rev. 6:8 in *Sermons Preached in Westminster Abbey,* (New York: W.J. Widdleton, 1860), 229.

4. Octavius Winslow (1808-1878), *Personal Declension & Revival of Religion in the Soul* (New York: Robert Cater, 1847).

5. C.H. Spurgeon (1834-1892), *Praying in the Holy Spirit*, Sermon No. 719 on Jude 1:20, 1866.

6. Edward Bickersteth (1786-1850), *Family Prayers* (Philadelphia: H. Hooker, 1843).

7. John Owen (1616-1683), "Pneumatologia or, A Discourse Concerning the Holy Spirit" in *The Works of John Owen*, vol. 3, Edited by W. Goold (Edinburg: T & T Clark, 1862). First pub. 1674.

8. Thomas Goodwin (1600-1680), "The Work of the Holy Ghost in Our Salvation" in *The Works of Thomas Goodwin*, vol. 6 (Edinburgh: Nichol, 1861).

9. Isaac Watts (1674-1748), *A Guide to Prayer*, 1715.

10. C.H. Spurgeon (1834-1892), *Our Urgent Need of the Holy Spirit*, Sermon No. 1332 on Rom. 15:13; 19, 1877.

11. John Bunyan (1628-1688), *Prayer* (originally two combined works: *The Spirit of Prayer* & *The Saints' Privilege and Profit*), First pub. 1662 & 1692 respectively.

12. Henry Law (1797-1884), *Family Prayers* (London: Nisbet, 1868).

13. Thomas Goodwin (1600-1680), "The Work of the Holy Ghost in Our Salvation" in *The Works of Thomas Goodwin*, vol. 6 (Edinburgh: Nichol, 1861).

14. Thomas Shepard (1605-1649), "Meditations & Spiritual Experiences" in *The Works of Thomas Shepard*, Vol. 3 (Boston: Doctrinal Tract and Book Society, 1853).

15. C.H. Spurgeon (1834-1892), *Receiving the Holy Spirit*, Sermon No. 1790 on Acts 19:2, 1884.

16. Richard Sibbes (1577-1635), "The Excellency of the Gospel Above the Law," a sermon on 1 Cor. 3:17-18 in *The Complete Works of Richard Sibbes*, vol. 4 (Edinburgh: James Nichol, 1863).

17. Richard Sibbes (1577-1635), "The Returning Backslider," Sermon No. 2 on Hos. 14:2 in *The Complete Works of Richard Sibbes*, vol. 2 (Edinburgh: James Nichol, 1862).

18. Edward Bickersteth (1786-1850), *Family Prayers* (Philadelphia: H. Hooker, 1843).

19. Andrew Murray (1828-1917), *The Prayer Life* (Abbotsford, WI: Aneko Press, 2018) 49. First pub. 1913.

20. John Owen (1616-1683), "A Discourse of the Work of The Holy Spirit in Prayer" in *The Works of John Owen*, vol. 4, Edited by W. Goold (Edinburg: T & T Clark, 1862). First pub. 1682.

21. Andrew Murray (1828-1917), *The Master's Indwelling*, 1895.

22. C.H. Spurgeon (1834-1892), *C.H. Spurgeon's Prayers* (Grand Rapids: Baker, 1978), 135.

23. Thomas Boston (1676-1732), "Discourses on Prayer" in *The Complete Works of* ..., vol. 11 (London: Tegg, 1853).

24. Ibid.

25. Andrew Murray (1828-1917), *The Master's Indwelling*, 1895.

26. F.B. Meyer (1847-1929), "The Spirit's Help" in *The Present Tenses of the Blessed Life*, 1892.

27. F.B. Meyer (1847-1929), "The Spirit's Help" in *The Present Tenses of the Blessed Life*, 1892.

28. John Owen (1616-1683), "A Discourse of the Work of The Holy Spirit in Prayer" in *The Works of John Owen*, vol. 4, Edited by W. Goold (Edinburg: T & T Clark, 1862). First pub. 1682.

29. C.H. Spurgeon (1834-1892), *The Holy Spirit's Intercession*, Sermon No. 1535 on Rom. 8:26-27, 1880.

30. Oliver Heywood (1630-1702), *Closet Prayer: A Christian Duty*, 1671.

31. Isaac Watts (1674-1748), "Breathing After the Holy Spirit" in *Hymns & Sacred Songs*. First pub. 1707.

32. Horatius Bonar (1808-1889), "Ch. 50: Unutterable Groans" in *Light and Truth (III): Acts and Larger Epistles*, 1869.

33. Oliver Heywood (1630-1702), *Closet Prayer: A Christian Duty*, 1671.

34. C.H. Spurgeon (1834-1892), *Our Urgent Need of the Holy Spirit*, Sermon No. 1332 on Rom. 15:13; 19, 1877.

35. Thomas Boston (1676-1732), "Discourses on Prayer" in *The Complete Works of* ..., vol. 11. (London: Tegg, 1853).

36. Isaac Watts (1674-1748), *A Guide to Prayer*, 1715.

37. Ibid.

38. C.H. Spurgeon (1834-1892), *The Holy Spirit's Intercession*, Sermon No. 1535 on Rom. 8:26-27, 1880.

39. A.B. Simpson (1843-1919), *The Life of Prayer*, 1890.

40. Isaac Watts (1674-1748), *A Guide to Prayer*, 1715.

41. Andrew Murray (1828-1917), *Why Do You Not Believe*, 1894.

42. Edward Bickersteth (1786-1850), *Family Prayers* (Philadelphia: H. Hooker, 1843).

43. Horatius Bonar (1808-1889), "Ch. 50: Unutterable Groans" in *Light and Truth (III): Acts and Larger Epistles*, 1869.

44. William Gurnall (1616-1679), "Praying Always" in *The Christian in Complete Armour*. 1662-1665.

45. Augustine of Hippo (354-430), "Psalm 119: Discourse XIV" on 119:25-48 in *Expositions of the Book of Psalms*.

46. Andrew Murray (1828-1917), *The Prayer Life* (Abbotsford, WI: Aneko Press, 2018) 48. First pub. 1913.

47. Octavius Winslow (1808-1878), "The Intercession of the Spirit in the Saints" in *No Condemnation in Christ Jesus*, 1852.

48. Horatius Bonar (1808-1889), "Ch. 50: Unutterable Groans" in *Light and Truth (III): Acts and Larger Epistles*, 1869.

49. William Gurnall (1616-1679), "Praying Always" in *The Christian in Complete Armour*. 1662-1665.

50. Horatius Bonar (1808-1889), "Unutterable Groans" in *Light and Truth (III): Acts and Larger Epistles*, 1869.

51. A.J. Gordon (1836-1895), *The Holy Spirit in Missions* (New York: Fleming H. Revell Co., 1893).

52. Henry Law (1797-1884), *Family Prayers* (London: Nisbet, 1868).

53. Horatius Bonar (1808-1889), "Unutterable Groans" in *Light and Truth (III): Acts and Larger Epistles*, 1869.

54. C.H. Spurgeon (1834-1892), *The Holy Spirit's Intercession*, Sermon No. 1535 on Rom. 8:26-27, 1880.

55. Octavius Winslow (1808-1878), "The Sympathy of the Spirit with the Infirmity of Prayer" in *No Condemnation in Christ Jesus*, 1852.

56. C.H. Spurgeon (1834-1892), *The Holy Spirit's Intercession*, Sermon No. 1535 on Rom. 8:26-27, 1880.

57. C.H. Spurgeon (1834-1892), *The Pastor in Prayer* (Edinburgh: Banner of Truth, 2004). Sourced from *The Pastor in Prayer* (Elliot Stock: London, 1893).

58. Thomas Boston (1676-1732), "Discourses on Prayer" in *The Complete Works of …*, vol. 11. (London: Tegg, 1853).

59. John Owen (1616-1683), "A Discourse of the Work of The Holy Spirit in Prayer" in *The Works of John Owen*, vol. 4, Edited by W. Goold (Edinburg: T & T Clark, 1862). First pub. 1682.

60. Thomas Boston (1676-1732), "Of the Rule of Direction in Prayer" in *The Complete Works of …*, vol. 2 (London: Tegg, 1853).

61. R.A. Torrey (1856-1928), *How to Pray*, 1900.

62. Isaac Watts (1674-1748), *A Guide to Prayer*, 1715.

63. John Owen (1616-1683), "A Discourse of the Work of The Holy Spirit in

Prayer" in *The Works of John Owen*, vol. 4, Edited by W. Goold (Edinburg: T & T Clark, 1862). First pub. 1682.

64. Henry Law (1797-1884), *Family Prayers* (London: Nisbet, 1868).

65. Thomas Manton (1620-1677), "Sermons Upon the Eighth Chapter of Romans: Sermon No. 35 on Rom. 8:26" in *The Complete Works of Thomas Manton*, vol. 12 (London: Nisbet, 1873).

66. Martin Luther (1483-1546), *Commentary on the Epistle to the Galatians*, 1535. Trans. by Theodore Graebner.

67. Anthony Burgess (1600-1663), "Sermon No. 135: Of a Humbled Christian Improving In His Prayers ..." on John 17:24 in *Christ's Prayer Before His Passion: Expository Sermons on John 17* (London: Abraham Miller, 1656).

68. Martin Luther (1483-1546), *Commentary on the Epistle to the Galatians*, 1535. Trans. by Theodore Graebner.

69. Edward Bickersteth (1786-1850), *Family Prayers* (Philadelphia: H. Hooker, 1843).

70. John Owen (1616-1683), "A Discourse of the Work of The Holy Spirit in Prayer" in *The Works of John Owen*, vol. 4, Edited by W. Goold (Edinburg: T & T Clark, 1862). First pub. 1682.

71. Andrew Murray (1828-1917), *The Prayer Life* (Abbotsford, WI: Aneko Press, 2018) 50. First pub. 1913.

72. C.H. Spurgeon (1834-1892), *The Holy Spirit's Chief Office*, Sermon No. 2382 on John 16:14-15, 1888.

73. Horatius Bonar (1808-1889), "Tract 13 (2): The Works of the Holy Spirit" in *The Kelso Tracts*, 1846.

74. Edward Bickersteth (1786-1850), *Family Prayers* (Philadelphia: H. Hooker, 1843).

75. Octavius Winslow (1808-1878), "Christ's Knowledge of His People" in *Fullness of Christ*, 1863.

76. Andrew Murray (1828-1917), *The Ministry of Intercession: A Plea for More Prayer*, 1898.

77. Ibid.

78. Richard Sibbes (1577-1635), "The Fountain Sealed," a sermon on Eph. 4:30 in *The Complete Works of Richard Sibbes*, vol. 5. (Edinburgh: James Nichol, 1863).

79. Isaac Watts (1674-1748), *A Guide to Prayer*, 1715.

80. William Jay (1769-1853), *Prayers for the Use of Families* (New York: Dodd & Mead, 1834).

81. George Whitefield (1714-1770), *A Continuation of the Reverend Mr.*

Whitefield's Journal: From His Arrival at London ..., 4th ed. (London: J. Hutton, 1739).

82. C.H. Spurgeon (1834-1892), *C.H. Spurgeon's Prayers* (Grand Rapids: Baker, 1978), 3-4.

83. Henry Law (1797-1884), *Family Prayers* (London: Nisbet, 1868).

84. Octavius Winslow (1808-1878), "The Intercession of the Spirit in the Saints" in *No Condemnation in Christ Jesus*, 1852.

Epilogue

1. Samuel Chadwick (1860-1932), quoted in *The New Encyclopedia of Christian Quotations* (Hampshire, UK: John Hunt Publishing, 2000), 783. Original source unknown.

2. Thomas Brooks (1608-1680), *The Privy Key of Heaven*, 1665.

3. William Gurnall (1616-1679), "Praying Always" in *The Christian in Complete Armour*. 1662-1665.

4. John Flavel (c.1627-1691), "The Third Meditation on Rom. 7:21" in *The Whole Works of* ..., vol. 6. (London: W. Baynes & Son, 1820).

5. Andrew Murray (1828-1917), *The Prayer Life* (Abbotsford, WI: Aneko Press, 2018) 140. First pub. 1913.

6. Gordon Watt (1865-1928), *Effectual Fervent Prayer* (Los Angeles: Biola Book Room, 1927)

7. Ibid.

8. R.A. Torrey (1856-1928), *How to Obtain Fullness of Power* (New York: Fleming H. Revell Co., 1897).

9. Andrew Murray (1828-1917), *The Prayer Life* (Abbotsford, WI: Aneko Press, 2018) 140. First pub. 1913.

10. Ibid., 142.

11. Ibid., 142.

12. Oliver Heywood (1630-1702), *Closet Prayer: A Christian Duty*, 1671.

13. Thomas Brooks (1608-1680), *The Privy Key of Heaven*, 1665.

Appendix Four

1. Thomas Brooks. *The Secret Key to Heaven: The Vital Importance of Private Prayer* (Carlisle, PA: Banner of Truth, 2006). First published in 1665 as *The Privy Key of Heaven*.

2. Oliver Heywood. *Private Prayer: A Christian Duty* (Westfield, IN: Digital Puritan Press, 2014). First published in 1671 as *Closet Prayer: A Christian Duty*.

3. William Gurnall. "Direction 11th: Praying Always" in *The Christian in Complete Armour: A Treatise of the Saint's War against the Devil* (Carlisle, PA: Banner of Truth, 1964). Vol. 2. First published 1662-1665.

4. Edward Bickersteth, *A Treatise on Prayer* (Schenectady, NY: A. Van Santvoord & M. Cole, 1822). First pub. 1819.

5. *Hindrances to Prayer*, Sermon No. 1192. *The Golden Key of Prayer* (No. 619), *Golden Vials Full of Odors* (No. 1051), *Order and Argument in Prayer* (No. 700), *A Call to Prayer & Testimony* (No. 2189), *True Prayer True Power* (No. 328), *Comfort for Those Whose Prayers are Feeble* (No. 3083), *The Holy Spirit's Intercession* (No. 1532)

6. Octavius Winslow, *The Works of Octavius Winslow (Portland, OR: Monergism, 2011).*

7. J. C. Ryle, *A Call to Prayer* (Carlisle, PA: Banner of Truth, 2002).

8. David McIntyre, *The Hidden Life of Prayer* (Tain, Scotland: Christian Focus, 2010)

9. Edward Bickersteth, *Family Prayers* (Philadelphia: H. Hooker, 1843).

10. Henry Law, *Family Prayers* (London: Nisbet, 1868).

11. Andrew Murray, *The Prayer Life* (Abbotsford, WI: Aneko Press, 2018) 114. First pub. 1913.

12. Albert Richardson, *The Kneeling Christian* (Louisville, KY: GLH Publishing, 2016).

13. Samuel Chadwick, *The Path of Prayer* (Fort Washington, PA: CLC Publications, 2000).

14. Octavius Winslow (1808-1878), "The Axe Laid to the Root" in *Glimpses of Truth As it Is in Jesus*, 1846.

Index to Quotes

Index of Authors by Date

The 4th -16th Century

Ambrose of Milan (c. 340-397)
John Chrysostom (347-407)
Augustine of Hippo (354-430)
Bernard of Clairvaux (1090-1153)
Anselm of Canterbury (c. 1033-1109)
Martin Luther (1483-1546)
John Calvin (1509-1564)
John Bradford (1510-1555)

The 17th-18th Century

Lewis Bayly (c. 1575-1631)
Richard Sibbes (1577-1635)
John Preston (1587-1628)
Jeremiah Burroughs (1599-1646)
William Bridge (c. 1600-1670)
Anthony Burgess (1600-1663)
Thomas Goodwin (1600-1680)
Isaac Ambrose (1604-1664)
Thomas Shepard (1605-1649)
Thomas Brooks (1608-1680)
Richard Alleine (1610-1681)
Robert Leighton (1611-1684)
Brother Lawrence (1614-1691)
Richard Baxter (1615-1691)
William Gurnall (1616-1679)
John Owen (1616-1683)
Thomas Manton (1620-1677)
Thomas Watson (1620-1686)
David Clarkson (1622-1686)
Samuel Lee (1625-1691)
William Bates (1625-1699)
George Swinnock (1627-1673)
John Flavel (c.1627-1691)

Stephen Charnock (1628-1680)
John Bunyan (1628-1688)
Oliver Heywood (1630-1702)
Philip Henry (1631-1696)
Nathaniel Vincent (c.1639-1697)
Benjamin Jenks (1646-1724)
Henry Scougal (1650-1678)
Matthew Henry (1662-1714)
Cotton Mather (1663-1728)
Thomas Ridgley (1667-1734)
Susanna Wesley (1669-1742)
Isaac Watts (1674-1748)
Thomas Boston (1676-1732
Philip Doddridge (1702-1751)
Jonathan Edwards (1703-1758)
Charles Wesley (1707-1788)
George Whitefield (1714-1770)
David Brainerd (1718-1747)
John Newton (1725-1807)
William Cowper (1731-1800)
Robert Hawker (1753-1827)
Samuel Knight (1759–1827)
William Wilberforce (1759-1833)
William Jay (1769-1853)
James Montgomery (1771-1854)
George Croly (1780-1860)
Edward Bickersteth (1786-1850)
Henry Lyte (1793-1847)
Henry Law (1797-1884)

The 19th - 20th Century

George Müller (1805-1898)
R. C. Trench (1807-1886)
Octavius Winslow (1808-1878)

Horatius Bonar (1808-1889)
Andrew Bonar (1810-1892)
Horatius Bonar (1808-1889)
Andrew Bonar (1810-1892)
Robert Murray M'Cheyne (1813-1843)
Fredrick W. Faber (1814-1863)
J.C. Ryle (1816-1900)
John MacDuff (1818-1895)
Joseph Scriven (1819-1886)
Alexander Maclaren (1826-1910)
Andrew Murray (1828-1917)
John Laidlow (1832-1906)
C.H. Spurgeon (1834-1892)
E.M. Bounds (1835-1913)
Frances R. Havergal (1836-1879)
A.J. Gordon (1836-1895)
Alexander Whyte (1836-1921)
A.T. Pierson (1837-1911)
Charitie L. (Smith) Bancroft (1841-1932)
A.B. Simpson (1843-1919)
F.B. Meyer (1847-1929)
James Hastings (1852-1922)

William M. Clow (1853-1930)
R.F. Horton (1855-1934)
R.A. Torrey (1856-1928)
S.D. Gordon (1859-1936)
David McIntyre (1859-1938)
Samuel Chadwick (1860-1932)
G. Campbell Morgan (1863-1945)
J.H. Jowett (1864-1923)
John "Praying" Hyde (1865-1912)
Gordon Watt (1865-1928)
Forbes Robinson (1867-1904)
Amy Carmichael (1867-1951)
Albert Richardson (1868-19__)
Oswald Chambers (1874-1917)
O. Hallesby (1879-1961)
J.O. Fraser (1886-1938)
A.W. Tozer (1897-1963)
Martyn Lloyd-Jones (1899-1981)
William E. Sangster (1900-1960)
J. Oswald Sanders (1902-1992)
Leonard Ravenhill (1907-1994)

Most Frequently Quoted

1. C.H. Spurgeon (1834-1892)
2. Octavius Winslow (1808-1878)
3. Andrew Murray (1828-1917)
4. Edward Bickersteth (1786-1850)
5. William Gurnall (1616-1679)
6. Thomas Manton (1620-1677)
7. Henry Law (1797-1884)
8. J.C. Ryle (1816-1900)
9. Oliver Heywood (1630-1702)
10. Thomas Boston (1676-1732)
11. A.B. Simpson (1843-1919)
12. Isaac Ambrose (1604-1664)
13. Thomas Brooks (1608-1680)
14. Richard Baxter (1615-1691)
15. George Swinnock (1627-1673)
16. Isaac Watts (1674-1748)
17. John Owen (1616-1683)

18. Horatius Bonar (1808-1889)
19. R.A. Torrey (1856-1928)
20. Andrew Bonar (1810-1892)
21. F.B. Meyer (1847-1929)
22. Martin Luther (1483-1546)
23. Lewis Bayly (c.1575-1631)
24. Benjamin Jenks (1646-1724)
25. J. Oswald Sanders (1902-1992)
26. Amy Carmichael (1867-1951)
27. Robert Leighton (1611-1684)
28. Samuel Chadwick (1860-1932)
29. David Clarkson (1622-1686)
30. Jonathan Edwards (1703-1758)
31. William Jay (1769-1853)
32. Alexander Maclaren (1826-1910)
33. G. Campbell Morgan (1863-1945)
34. Martyn Lloyd-Jones (1899-1981)

$\mathcal{D}$elighting
IN THE WORD

Don't miss this series of fully inductive Bible studies for women from Keri Folmar!

Loved by churches. Endorsed by Kristi Anyabwile, Connie Dever, Gloria Furman, Kathleen Nielson, and Diane Schreiner.

Currently six volumes—the book of Romans coming soon!

10 weeks	*10 weeks*	*10 weeks*
		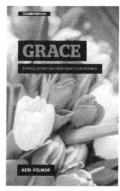
Joy! (Philippians)	*Faith* (James)	*Grace* (Ephesians)

11 weeks	*11 weeks*	*9 weeks*

Son of God (Gospel of Mark, 2 volumes)   *Zeal* (Titus)

bit.ly/DITWstudies

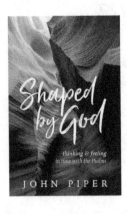

Shaped by God
Thinking and Feeling in Tune with the Psalms

John Piper | 86 pages

The Psalms are not just commanding... they are contagious.

bit.ly/ShapedbyGod

Wilderness Wanderings
Finding Contentment in the Desert Times of Life

Stacy Reaoch
Foreword by Jani Ortlund | 120 pages

25 devotionals for women reflecting on our journey to the Promised Land

bit.ly/wilwand

Brass Heavens
Reasons for Unanswered Prayer

Paul Tautges | 112 pages

Does it ever seem like God is not listening? Scripture offers six clear reasons why your prayers may go unanswered.

bit.ly/BRASS-H

The Scars That Have Shaped Me
How God Meets Us in Suffering

Vaneetha Rendall Risner
Foreword by Joni Eareckson Tada | 200 pages

She begged God for grace that would deliver her. But God offered something better: his sustaining grace.

bit.ly/THESCARS

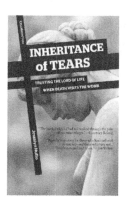

Inheritance of Tears
Trusting the Lord of Life When Death Visits the Womb

Jesssalyn Hutto | 95 pages

Miscarriage: deeply traumatic, tragically common, too often misunderstood.

bit.ly/OFTEARS

Grieving, Hope and Solace
When a Loved One Dies in Christ

Albert N. Martin | 112 pages

There is comfort for the grief. There are answers to the questions.

bit.ly/GriefHope

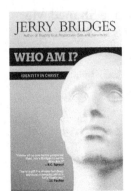

Who Am I?
Identity in Christ

Jerry Bridges | 91 pages

Jerry Bridges unpacks Scripture to give the Christian eight clear, simple, interlocking answers to one of the most essential questions of life.

bit.ly/WHOAMI

The Company We Keep
In Search of Biblical Friendship

Jonathan Holmes
Foreword by Ed Welch | 112 pages

Biblical friendship is deep, honest, pure, tranparent, and liberating. It is also attainable.

bit.ly/B-Friend

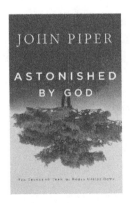

Astonished by God
Ten Truths to Turn the World Upside Down

John Piper | 192 pages

Turn your world on its head.

bit.ly/AstonishedbyGod

Two books by Peter Krol

Knowable Word
*Helping Ordinary People
Learn to Study the Bible
(Revised and Expanded)*
bit.ly/Knowable

Sowable Word
*Helping Ordinary People
Learn to Lead Bible
Studies*
bit.ly/Sowable

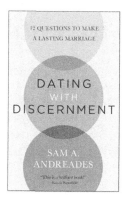

Dating with Discernment
12 Questions to Make a Lasting Marriage

Sam A. Andreades | 280 pages

A fresh, biblical paradigm for choosing a spouse.

"This is a brilliant book!" – Rosaria Butterfield
"Profoundly insightful" – Joel R. Beeke

bit.ly/DatingWell

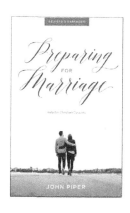

Preparing for Marriage
Help for Christian Couples

John Piper | 86 pages

*As you prepare for marriage, dare to dream
with God.*

bit.ly/prep-for-marriage

Run to Win:
The Lifelong Pursuits of a Godly Man

Tim Challies | 163 pages

Plan to run, train to run…run to win.

bit.ly/RUN2WIN

Do More Better
A Practical Guide to Productivity

Tim Challies | 114 pages

Don't try to do it all. Do more good. Better.

bit.ly/domorebetter

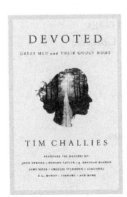

Devoted
Great Men and Their Godly Moms

Tim Challies | 128 pages

Women shaped the men who changed the world.

bit.ly/devotedbook

Made in the USA
Monee, IL
03 December 2023